The Sacred Bridge Within

A Tale of Awakening

W. L. Blossom

For Samuel, Isaac & Emma

All images are the creations of Bahman Farzad,

A brilliant and beautiful light in the world.

May his visions always be treasured.

1944 - 2016

Imagine you are the sky, the oceans, the mountains

and the breeze,

while knowing you are comprised of the planets

and every star in the heavens.

Infinity lies within you.

Table of Contents

Prologue

Chapter 1: Remembering	1
Chapter 2: The Love	23
Chapter 3: The Chief	41
Chapter 4: The Heart	61
Chapter 5: The Earth	81
Chapter 6: The Moon	111
Chapter 7: The Rock	133
Chapter 8: The Witness	161
Chapter 9: Shinkyo	181

Prologue

I would call myself a skeptic, when it comes to New Age hype and tend to be quite logical in how I live my life.

And yet I remember being on Earth far beyond my years.

I am often aware of other dimensions simultaneously and recall various cycles of evolution here.

In fact, I remember simply being the light of consciousness and the eons leading up to our present devolved awareness.

But as you can imagine, I wasn't always like this.

I grew up in a small college town, immersed in academia, in contrast to my life at home of daily devotions and strict attendance to our neighborhood church.

From a young age, I envisioned myself engaged in mission work, devoting my time to saving the lost and suffering in the world.

Little did I realize, how dramatically my perspective would depart from inherited views.

When I was a young adult, I was deeply traumatized.

My pulse completely stopped as my awareness rose out of my body and the life force gently left me.

As I ascended into the sky, the ceiling became holographic as did the world around me.

I instinctively knew, I was transitioning out of my physical life.

I was at last at peace, without a care or concern.

I was in a state of euphoria that felt inherent to me.

As I looked down at my crumpled body lying on the floor, I watched my small children playing in the rooms below me.

And from this unusual vantage point of exceptional clarity, I paused to consider my options, then chose to return to the life I'd created and finish my journey here.

In doing so, I returned to a new reality.

Ever since, I've lived in a world that is foreign to my brain, similar to that described in schools of awakening, yet it seems to happily co-exist with my logical mind, such as witnessing the energy fields of which the world is comprised.

But for those without my experience, how does one relate?

Even for me, after decades of insights, many questions remain.

How can we ever know if perceptions beyond the logical mind are simply being imagined or true in some regard?

When we remember past lifetimes, did they really exist?

Were they truly our own?

Or are we tapping into some kind of collective memory?

Do we have the ability to assimilate forms of alternative consciousness healing for ourselves?

Are intuitive visions simply nature's biofeedback loop that guides, heals and reprograms the damaged human psyche?

Or are they just the random contents of the subconscious mind?

How much do we truly know about our existence, anyway?

Whatever the case may be, I have found exceptional healing within my clarity with the release of past residue and negative frequencies.

And I have learned that data stored in our physicality greatly impacts our lives on Earth by encoding our energy fields with electromagnetic frequencies, based on the contents of the conscious, subconscious and unconscious mind, along with other filters such as cellular programming and of course, our DNA.

Freedom from these frequencies is the key to awakening.

The following tale is verbatim my own experience.

All events and conversations are taken from my journals.

My journey reveals a side of myself, I rarely disclose in my life.

May it be a catalyst for others' enlightenment.

Author's Note…

I am writing this thirty years after my awakening began, and in retrospect, I understand my experiences far better.

Although I resonate deeply with ancient philosophies, I attribute my own past life recall to collective memory accessed via nonlinear time by merging with a particular person in human history from whom I might find personal healing or gain more clarity, despite each past life feeling as if, it was truly my own at the time.

Carl Jung referred to this vast storehouse as 'the universal psyche' in which we can fully immerse ourselves for bits of wisdom and healing.

So in retrospect, I see my 'past lives' as healing modalities and do not identify in this life as anyone, but me.

But I also know, we are each a blend of possibilities…

So then again, who knows…

Chapter One

Remembering

At the risk of sounding dramatic, is it fair to say that divorce is akin to ending your own life, regarding the hopes and dreams your marriage once conjured for you?

I used to think of my own divorce as ritual seppuku - the self-inflicted disembowelment of the ancient samurai - in the face of defeat, they died by their own hand with heroic courage and honor.

I remember having this same attitude when confronted with divorce and fully committing to executing a swift and complete dissolution.

But afterward, came a much bigger challenge that hadn't occurred to me. How do we fully recover from ultimate defeat?

How do we reinvent ourselves socially, emotionally, spiritually and economically?

And how do we resist the temptation of future hyperbole?

I asked myself these questions many years ago as I sank into a quiet state of confusion and utter despair.

Though, I didn't know the entirety of the answers I would receive, there appeared a silver-lining; my disembowelment was complete.

Metaphorically, I examined the entrails now in front of me, astonished by the amount of garbage the human body can hold, but most of all, I was relieved, they were no longer rotting inside me.

Life's trauma can be re-directive as a catalyst for change.

I was backed into a corner, where there appeared to be no escape, so with the passion and conviction of a kamikaze pilot, I committed to fixing myself, come what may.

A further insight came one day while visiting a friend, who listened to me whine for as long as he could stand it, then looked me in the eye and declared, "You cause all your problems!"

At first, this new information sounded like scrambled gibberish. But as my mind began to grasp the statement's full meaning, a light of revelation flared deep inside of me.

If indeed, I cause my problems… surely, I can stop causing them.

This astonished me!

As my friend sent my sorry ass packing that day with a "Free Psychic Reading" card, he grabbed from his kitchen counter, I stepped into a whole new world in which I could change myself.

At home, I dialed the number on the card and scheduled an appointment. Later that day, I was shaking hands with my first clairvoyant.

This was a new experience for me, one I hadn't considered before, yet I'd exhausted my traditional options and figured anything goes. More than a little tentative, I sat back in my chair as the 'reading' began.

The woman in front of me knowingly smiled, then closed her twinkling eyes as she began 'tuning into' me.

I silently braced myself.

"You have a past lifetime lighting up," she began. "You were a sturdy, hardworking woman living in a little fishing village along the coast of Italy."

"Huh," I quietly murmured, not particularly impressed.

"In another life, you were a small boy living in the jungles of Africa, relying solely on your intuition for survival," she said next.

That was a bit scary. I couldn't imagine it.

"And once, you were a young man in the closest circle of Jesus' friends during his life on Earth," she said with emphasis.

"Oh really?" I questioned politely as her final suggestion struck me as completely ridiculous.

Later at home, I thought of my reading and what it had meant to me. At first, it seemed preposterous and almost embarrassing.

But slowly, my foremost impression became a deep sense of wonder and peace.

In fact, it awoke a sense of self far greater than I'd ever known. At the time, I didn't appreciate it, but it served as a positive data point.

Either way, I wasn't ready for this far-out psychic stuff, so I put my reading experience into the 'things that are a little too weird for me' compartment in my memory bank, and life went on.

* * *

A year later, I was miserable. I'd survived a crushing divorce and my kids were settling into our new dynamic at home, but I still felt a long way from happiness. No matter the everyday circumstances, I remained profoundly sad.

So with nowhere else to turn, I thought of a new plan; I would fix myself from the inside as every attempt on the outside had been surprisingly unsuccessful.

One day, I thought of the audio tape the clairvoyant had given to me. She said it might heal my broken heart, which peaked my curiosity.

"Christian Meditation," the label read.

Intrigued, I decided to open it and in doing so, I took a step in a new direction that day.

I sat down in a comfy chair in my living room, closed my eyes and took a deep breath out of nervousness.

Then I quietly listened as the voice on the tape began, first with gentle music, followed by narrative:

"Sit up straight in a quiet place... focus in the center of your head... open your foot chakras to let in earth energy... let the energy move up your leg channels and into your first chakra... then back down your grounding cord to the center of the earth."

"Now bring cosmic energy in through your crown chakra at the top of your head... down your back channels... mix this cosmic energy with the earth energy running through your first chakra... run the mixture up your front channels... and let it fountain out the top of your head... filling your aura with divinely healing energy and...."

"Okay," I laughed as the tape continued, still searching for 'the center of your head' as the first of many new concepts.

But day after day, I stuck with it. Soon, I began to get it.

Little by little, I noticed myself gaining fragments of clarity.

Time after time, I 'sat' within my deepening consciousness as the experience became more tactile.

I could feel the energies moving within me, like a cozy, cosmic jacuzzi mixed with the wellness of Mother Earth igniting a whole new sense of self I never knew existed.

* * *

Making the commitment to heal can be profoundly healing in itself.

On the eleventh day of my new meditation practice, something unimaginable happened to me; I met 'God.'

Now, I know that sounds unbelievable, and maybe it sounds insane, but I also know there are others, who have experienced the same. Here's what happened...

I sat perfectly still, trying for the umpteenth time to be in the center of my head, while running my earth and cosmic energies, feeling overwhelmed with the complexity of my new meditation practice.

On top of it all, my mind began chattering, "Dear God, help me learn how to meditate and end my misery!"

Then without thinking, I did something that I had never conceived of before; I simply shut up and somehow, I completely silenced my brain.

I hadn't figured anything out, I just shut up for no reason at all and sat perfectly still and listened, when a truly wondrous and radiant light appeared above my eyes that swirled inside me and filled my darkness with pure and perfect love.

I 'knew' it was God.

I couldn't explain it.

I just knew it with 'a knowingness that surpasses all understanding.'

God's presence was so magnificent, I was overwhelmed. It affected me so profoundly that I burst into tears and sobbed at the thought that God would bother to acknowledge my meager and downtrodden soul.

The experience only lasted 5-10 seconds and yet, it was an experience that transformed me from a person of faith to a person of absolute knowing.

Instantly, I knew that God truly exists as pure and powerful love, and the source of all existence.

Could this really be it?

I called my friend who had sent my sorry ass packing the year before.

"There really is a God!" I exploded.

"I know, isn't it cool?" he said.

It was all so unbelievable, yet somehow, it felt divine.

And surprisingly, it rang true to me in my logical mind.

For several days, I was in an uncanny state of awareness.

I saw myself in imagery; a tall, slender, intricately painted vase, dark blue on one side and light on the other with tiny white flowers throughout.

I saw this elegant vessel as representative of my earthly existence, buried under a mountain of pain, grief and fear.

Then as my new awareness filled me in the present, this vessel of earthly existence exploded from within, freeing me from a timeless tomb of human suffering.

Naked, I stood in the light of the sun, beyond my physical form, gazing across the shattered pieces of my subconscious mind.

They lay scattered beyond the horizon.

Deeply inhaling the fresh air for the first time in a very long time, I felt the warmth of the sun on my skin.

I felt released.

I felt fresh and new.

I experienced my divinity.

I could see people's energy fields with pictures and encoding. In fact, I could see their ethereal essence with perfect clarity.

I was captivated by the profundity of my new perspective on Earth, but most of all the realization that it was inherent in me.

Then, much to my chagrin, after several days, my super-charged state of awareness faded away and I came back to whom I had been before being 'filled with The Holy Spirit.'

No matter how hard I tried, I couldn't replicate it.

Yet the experience was now deeply rooted in my self awareness.

Excited about my new revelations, I visited my church and shared the details of my experience with my childhood pastor, expecting affirmation or something positive.

Instead, he nervously backed away and crushed my heartfelt confession.

"You must have had a complete psychotic breakdown," he said.

"Not at all," I responded, surprised by this. "Don't you see? I know, God is real!"

"That's impossible," he insisted, then began to ramble, nonsensically, about social order, salvation and our separation from God in a mix of academic perspectives disclosing his own ambivalence.

But despite his unexpected reaction, I knew my perceptions were 'real' as a deeper faith and trust in myself organically appeared.

So I continued to meditate daily, which felt like trying to move a mountain, one handful at a time. And yet, I knew I was making progress, albeit very slowly.

* * *

At this point in my journey, I began to question my faith.

Why are there so many religions with such complexity?

And why is there so much dissension about the concept of God in the world? Are religions truly divine? Or are they just the projections of the controlling human mind?

In fact, religion reminded me of a game I played as a child.

"The Telephone Game" is played in a circle. A story is whispered around. As the story is passed from one child to the next with each teller's unique perspective, it often morphs into something different from the original tale.

At the end of the game, everyone laughs, when they hear the original version retold in contrast to the last.

However, when it comes to religion, few people are laughing today, despite the 'truths' of any religion originating from oral traditions retold over thousands of years.

* * *

As my new awareness brought me fully into the present, a greater depth of clarity blossomed somewhere inside of me.

I didn't realize it at the time, but I was beginning to 'see as spirit.'

Unaware, I continued my quest to find a morsel of peace within.

But the road was long and the march was tough. With all its peaks and valleys, it hardly seemed worth it at times.

One day, I thought of the bible verse, "Be still and know that I am God" which sparked an interest in the quiet practice of Buddhist meditation.

In contrast to running energies from the heavens and the earth, Buddhist meditation cultivates stillness deep within.

So every day I sat in silence for an hour or more, in an empty state of consciousness, similar to a void.

This brought with it many wonderful changes and many challenging times, and around every corner, a new level of healing began.

"How could I have so much pain and sorrow in my brief 40 years?" I asked one day in exasperation.

This made no sense to me.

So I looked up to the heavens and admitted to defeat.

"Okay, now what?" I conceded.

And with this, I fully surrendered to 'that which lies within' as the veil between heaven and earth fell away.

Thus began my awakening.

* * *

The spring brought with it a new breed of teacher I instinctively knew was divine. Helena taught Kundalini Yoga at The Center for Happiness.

I was drawn to the yoga studio for its peaceful energies, but most of all, I was drawn to the word 'kundalini.'

It's one of those words that tickles as it dances over your tongue, like periwinkle or dandelion. I simply fell in love with the word and often delighted in saying it... "k-u-n-d-a-l-i-n-i."

As the first flowers of spring broke through the dormant, snow-covered ground, I began my yoga practice.

Pleased to have found a yoga center within a short commute, I began practicing kundalini yoga on a weekly basis, thereby increasing the life force energy fueling my own unique presence.

Perhaps I had finally found a place where I could truly belong.

Later that summer, I went to a workshop Helena had arranged. It focused on a contemplative form of healing oneself and others.

The visiting guru of 'Sat Nam Rasayan' was the world's foremost teacher regarding this ancient energy work.

Sat Nam Rasayan is directly translated as 'deep relaxation in the true identity' which may be achieved in 'Shuniya' - a state of inner stillness at zero-point frequency.

This level of human consciousness fosters expansive compassion and optimal clarity.

Esoteric powers are said to exist at this 'non-frequency.'

I had never met a guru nor given the concept much thought, but my curious nature and love of adventure opened my mind to receive instruction from this benevolent soul.

Hours later, the session ended with a gong meditation, a gentle rhythm meant to lull one into deep relaxation.

And during this gong meditation, I remembered my first past lifetime completely on my own.

The pulse of this ancient instrument had opened a door to nonlinear time and to visions that came without warning. The memory was so familiar, it caught me by surprise.

As I relaxed on my yoga cushion, I experienced myself as a young woman in India, thousands of years ago.

I appeared to be very delicate, with a much slighter physical form than I have today. I was wearing a bright, blue sari made of fine silk with tiny white blossoms embroidered throughout.

My skin was bronze, my eyes were dark and my ebony hair flowed down my back in a luxurious cascade. It too, was bejeweled with little white flowers to match my elegant attire.

As I walked through an open-air pavilion, in what I knew was a university setting, the hot Indian sun warmed my skin and a breeze of exotic spices filled the humid air.

The barely detectable nuance of sounds and sensations poured into me like a distant memory, though it felt not distant at all.

And I knew of my life in India, as I know of my life today.

I was living a life of privilege and highly educated for a woman of the time. I had grown up with Siddhartha Gautama, a distant cousin and friend.

We shared a happy childhood together, playing beside the reflection pool within the garden walls.

Instinctively, I fast-forwarded the vision to my adolescence.

"I honor the divinity within you," we often greeted one another beside the reflection pool.

Then I watched as we grew older and he was called, 'The Enlightened One.'

Years later, I witnessed his passing, not long before my own.

We had shared a deep affinity and parted as dear friends.

On the day the blossoms fell from the trees, I sat by his side as he peacefully smiled and left the world behind.

As the rhythm of the gong slowly faded, I found myself lying in the soft light of the classroom again.

Those around me began to stir, but I remained transfixed.

I was stunned by the absolute clarity of the life I'd experienced, living it as my own while observing myself within it.

Unlike something imagined, the memories were even clearer than my drive to the workshop that day. And the mode by which I 'remembered' them felt eerily reminiscent to my questioning brain.

Then as my mind slowly re-engaged, I was filled with many thoughts.

Do past lifetimes really exist? Are they truly our own? If so, do we have the ability to transcend present time in the world to experience them again?

I still wasn't convinced.

And where do the memories come from? Are they stored in the subconscious mind or collective memory? Did they really happen to us or are they simply a nonlinear, healing modality?

Either was I didn't identify with any past life I'd seen, but felt extremely grateful to glean bits of wisdom from them.

* * *

In January of the following year, Helena offered a class called, "Higher Consciousness Training."

The class included a book by Dr. Brian Weiss, a Yale-trained psychiatrist, traditionally versed in Freudian theory.

He had written a book called, "Many Lives, Many Masters," after witnessing spontaneous past life recall in patients under hypnosis.

I read this and his subsequent books, looking for clues to explain my blossoming past life awareness.

In one of these books, "Mirrors of Time," I found a CD in the back that leads the reader through a past life regression. I could hardly wait to try it.

The next morning, I settled into a cozy chair in my living room. I took a deep breath and closed my eyes as I opened my inner awareness.

The CD led me through a relaxation exercise in which I envisioned myself going down a long, winding flight of stairs, a visualization technique meant to lead one deeper and deeper into their own subconscious mind.

There, in the depths of my being, I stood before a mirror in which I saw my unique reflection.

And just as curious Alice once stepped through the looking glass, so did I step through my own image and into a meadow of tall, waving grass in a place all too familiar.

The wildflower meadow was south of the place in which I had grown up. But the quaint little town of my present-day life didn't exist at all. Instead, I found myself at home in a tranquil village of teepees.

I was a young woman, tall and slender with long, straight, dark hair. I wore a simple dress tied at the waist with a twisted belt.

Not far away, my two small children played by the meadow's stream. My son was three, strong and brave. My daughter was younger, but wise for her years.

It was a clear autumn day, reminiscent of the summer sun.

The village was humming with routine activities as the women preserved the food they had gathered and grown for the seasons to come, while the men were out hunting.

Then without warning, a band of braves appeared from the woods beyond. I called to my children, who looked my way as I dropped my basket of work and ran swiftly toward them.

A painted brave on horseback struck a lethal blow.

With outstretched arms, I let out a call unlike any other, but the cry from a mother's heart, as I watched my son and daughter struck beyond my reach.

I lay in the sweet autumn grass as the smoke from the burning village filled the air and dimmed the sun that had warmed my skin just moments before, and I was gone.

As the life force gently left me, I lovingly swept my children up into their mother's arms, securely embracing them as we ascended beyond the physical realm.

When I returned from this lucid memory, I was struck by the detail again; the sounds, the smells, the warmth of the sun and the smoke from the burning village as it caught my final breath.

My interest was piqued by the realization that despite the violent end to our lives, we'd experienced a neutral passing.

* * *

Now at this time in my journey, I felt rejuvenated.

I embraced empowerment.

I was going through major paradigm shifts on all levels now and beginning to experience past lifetimes as real. Despite my continued skepticism, I was receiving therapeutic benefit from them.

I noticed that unresolved energies can remain in our energy fields when we reincarnate within the earthly realm. They are retained as subtle frequencies on a cellular level.

These remnants of emotion can trigger knee-jerk reactions to people and situations we wouldn't normally choose, affecting our lives in various ways via the countless layers of the manifest human mind (the filters through which we project and perceive our realities in this realm).

Therefore, it only seemed logical that releasing these past life energies could be healing and even transformative on many significant levels (even as a placebo, which science suggests can improve results by 30% - 70%).

So with the delicate hands of a divine surgeon, I began extracting countless, karmic gems from my energy field, deeming them as no longer beneficial for me in the present.

And with this simple process, my vibration slowly increased as I began to carry far less subconscious debris.

Could the awareness of this vast karmic warehouse stored within ourselves engender a deeper sense of compassion for everyone else in the world?

* * *

Later, I sat down to meditate and another regression began as I shifted into a new dimension in which I hadn't yet been.

The portal through which I passed didn't lead to a past life at all, but to the ethereal plane, where I experienced myself as the infinite being from which my awareness originates.

I looked very different as my 'Higher Self.' I was larger than I would imagine, like a giant playing with a finger puppet compared to my body on Earth.

And I was struck by my radiant countenance - comprised of heavenly light. I had almond eyes, an aquiline nose, beautiful lips and long, silky hair. A wisp of golden energy connected my iridescent presence to my physical form.

'God' stood before me with arms opened wide.

"This is your path, my dear one," he said. "You must trust in what you are seeing one hundred percent."

* * *

During another day of Higher Consciousness Training, I was filled with wonder and awe, basking in the afterglow of a guided meditation.

Marina, a gifted healer, was our guest speaker that day. She had channeled a new technique and was sharing it with the class.

Through a series of clearings and downloads, she was able to help others disconnect from 'the collective shadow' - humanity's low vibration currently smothering the world.

Once released, they could rise above this collective ceiling and easily shift their vibration to a much higher frequency.

Energy grids are the means by which we manifest presence on Earth. Elevating the frequency of your personal energy field allows you to hold a higher vibration in your ethereal form.

And the higher your vibration, the more easily you can create your optimal life in the world.

This process greatly intrigued me, so in mid-July, I met privately with Marina.

After greeting one another and making a cup of tea, I told her I'd been recalling past lives and other surprising things.

And much to my amazement, Marina didn't roll her eyes or even laugh at me, but sat quietly and listened.

Then she said a blessing and looked at me with a comforting smile as she raised her glance above me, as if looking somewhere else.

I was puzzled at first, then realized she was conversing with my Higher Self, telepathically.

"You're in a major shift right now," Marina explained to me. "The facet that has been you on Earth, the one that experiences lessons here, is on its way out. Two new facets are coming in; your Galactic and Native American facets."

Then she took a sip of tea as I tried to process this.

"You're moving to a frequency beyond basic healing now," she continued. "You're shifting to a higher vibration. All your gifts as a Native American healer are moving into your energy field. This will greatly deepen your connection with Mother Earth."

"Your Galactic and Inter-dimensional facets, are merging with you too. They will help you achieve your next phase in the physical world."

"You are not to sell your home on Sanibel Island," she relayed from my Higher Self. "You will live there, someday. The money is on the way."

Several years before this, during my divorce, I met with the court-elected official determining child custody.

At our meeting, we visited over a glass-covered table of shells. Despite the stress of the interview, I couldn't take my eyes off the delicate little treasures.

When I asked, where she had found them, the woman replied, "Sanibel."

The word rang out like music. I was completely charmed. So I tracked it down and took a trip. I knew Sanibel Island was where I belonged.

I walked on the beach for hours on end as the warm island sun, salt on the breeze and sounds of the ocean replenished my soul. I began to save every penny to buy an island home.

Years later, I made my dream come true with work and diligence.

But not long after I purchased it, the home was struck by Hurricane Charlie and shortly thereafter, Katrina. I was forced to hire attorneys to defend my insurance claim as the cavalry-image I held of insurers became a villainous one.

They stalled in court for several years. In the end, they never paid. So I put the home on the market, not knowing what else to do.

"I've lost everything with the hurricanes," I confessed to Marina that day.

"I understand," she responded as something in my energy field noticeably caught her attention. "But you should know, my dear one, your fortunes will soon change."

Chapter Two

The Love

By the summer, my life began to feel somewhat normal again, but with my shifts in perspective, 'normal' was redefined.

One evening, I met with old college friends. Annie was getting remarried the following week. I would be her attendant and Patricia would do her hair.

As we sat on Annie's porch, she raised her glass of wine.

"Here's to the man who beat Jake," Annie robustly declared.

"Who?" I asked with surprise.

"You remember Jake, he was in college with us," Annie explained.

I hadn't heard that name in over twenty years.

Then despite my vague recollection of many things in life, a flood of memories came to me, including freshman French with Jake and his hint at a future proposal.

"What's so special about him?" asked Patricia, bringing me back from the past.

"Since college, I've thought of Jake as the quintessential man," Annie explained. "I've used his exceptional character as a measuring stick for all other men."

"You know, now that I think of it," I playfully chimed in. "He seemed to sparkle whenever he smiled, in fact, he was mesmerizing!"

"Well then," said Patricia, raising her glass of wine. "Let's hear it for all the mesmerizing men around the world."

And our conversation went on.

The next night, I went back to Annie's for more preparation and plans. Just for fun, Annie called Jake to ask if he'd be at her wedding.

"Are you coming to my wedding next week?" she playfully asked. "Yes, I know you were here last month. Of course, I understand."

Then after a pause, she tried again.

"Guess who will be my attendant?" she asked in a mischievous tone. "Okay, see you next week!"

Annie hung up the phone with astonishment in her eyes.

"Somehow, he guessed it was you, and instantly changed his mind," she declared.

"Oh my gosh!" the two of us squealed in girlish unison as my mind began to race.

"I can't believe he just said that..." a voice chattered inside my brain. "I wonder what he looks like after so many years... oh no, even worse... think of what I look like!"

"Seriously?" Annie interrupted. "He's coming, because of you!"

I began to feel self conscious as Annie continued to speak.

"Did I tell you what happened last month, when he was visiting?" she asked.

I shook my head.

"We ran into our daughters downtown," Annie began. "They were sitting on the bench in front the coffee shop. He'd met my daughter earlier, so just for fun, I pointed to your's and asked, "Guess who this is?"

"She has her mother's beautiful eyes," he said without missing a beat."

"What?" I exclaimed as my jaw hit the floor. "He said, he remembers my eyes?"

An hour later, the telephone rang, it was Jake again. He'd thrown his invitation away and needed wedding details.

Annie began to fill him in, when the doorbell rang.

"Here, take this," she insisted, shoving the phone in my face.

"Hello," I said in a tentative voice.

"Is this who I think it is?" Jake playfully asked.

"Last time I checked," I volleyed, my sassiness instantly back. "Is this who I think it is?"

"It is," he robustly declared.

Instantly, I gave into my timeless affection for this man.

A half hour later, Annie returned.

"Give me that!" she demanded as I relinquished the phone.

The next day, I thought about Jake. I wondered why I was drawn to him after so many years. My past life regressions had given me insight into who I was and why, so I decided to try an experiment.

I wanted to see if I could direct a past life regression to a lifetime in which I had known Jake. Could there have possibly been one?

So I sat down in a quiet place, took a deep breath and closed my eyes. With laser focus, I turned my attention deep inside myself.

"How am I connected to Jake?" I quietly postulated.

Instantly, a past lifetime lit up.

It was the mid-16th century, Jake and I lived between Italy and France, I could see our locale on the map. We lived on the border between the two countries, halfway up from the coast.

We considered ourselves neither French nor Italian, but somewhere in between. We spoke both languages fluently, but our language of choice was French.

We played together as children and lived on neighboring farms.

As adolescents, our friendship deepened, until we fell in love. Eventually we married, and shortly thereafter, our children arrived.

With a jolt, the vision stopped as I stared in disbelief.

The children we had in that lifetime were the children I have today.

"How is that even possible?" my mind grappled with the implications, then decided to go along with the energies swirling around in my brain.

And as the portal remained, I witnessed the course of our lives. It was the happiest lifetime I had seen thus far.

Then, I remembered his curious question during this present life.

It was the fall of our sophomore year in college, our first walk together and first conversation alone.

"What would you say, if I asked you to marry me?" he sweetly said out of the blue.

His question was so unexpected, it caught me by surprise. Somewhat befuddled, I paused for an instant, then shrugged and answered, "No."

* * *

As I began to remember past lives, I recognized people in them. Even though their appearance had changed from one lifetime to the next, their soul had remained the same.

Somehow, I always recognized them when I looked into their eyes.

Jake's decision to come to the wedding wasn't just about me, it was about the kids as well. Jake was once their father, albeit unfathomably.

Then I thought of the day Jake met my daughter in front of the coffee shop and knew there's more to the eyes than mere physicality.

Had Jake remembered our beautiful daughter, while looking into her eyes?

A few days later, I found myself back on the spiritual plane. My Galactic and Native American facets stood before me as if introducing themselves. I smiled and embraced them without hesitation as we merged into 'One.'

Now a decade into my journey, I was committed to finding that place, where our true identity lies. And admittedly, there were many times when I thought, perhaps, I'd arrived. But just as climbing a mountain gives a view of yet another mountain to climb, so it seems with healing.

* * *

A week later, I felt fear burbling up regarding Jake.

We were having a pre-wedding get together.

I was a bundle of nerves.

As I was getting ready that evening, the mirror before me vanished as a scene appeared in its place. There was Jake, as large as life, walking through the vision where the mirror had just been as a tall, slender and very strong, aboriginal man.

He had bronze skin, dark shoulder length hair, bleached by the sun to a chocolate-brown. He was barefoot and bare-bodied, except for a loin cloth at his waist.

He was naturally rugged, yet surprisingly refined and I knew I was seeing him as he had been when humans first seeded the planet.

"Whoa, this is surreal," I thought as I took a step back.

But the surreal quality of the vision wasn't the portal at all, it was the palpable, timeless reality that it revealed in the present.

Then Jake traversed out of the vision as the portal closed, and I finished getting ready to go.

Shortly thereafter, I sat down to take a closer look. As I stepped through the portal from which the vision had come, Jake was there to greet me.

I remembered our unified presence and infinite consciousness, before humanity sank into a fractured sense-of-self.

We instinctively lived in harmony with all existence on Earth as the indigenous people seeded all over the planet.

And I knew, this past life had appeared to assure me that all would be well.

I saw Jake later that night. I was walking along the river and talking on my phone. Jake and friends pulled up next to me in a silver jeep.

"Oh my God, she looks exactly the same," he said behind the rolled up window, not knowing I could 'hear' him.

As he rolled the window down, we reached for each other's hand, saying "hello" in unison with shy, familiar smiles.

He hadn't changed over the years, time had served him well and added a depth to his energy field not noticeable in his youth.

I adored him beyond measure and couldn't wait to catch up.

* * *

The day of the wedding arrived. After the ceremony, I assisted the bride with various tasks until the guests had gone, then followed the newlyweds to the reception hall across town.

By the time our party arrived, all the guests had taken their seats. I scanned the expansive ballroom for a vacant chair and noticed a spot next to Jake and other college friends.

Suddenly, I felt shy about asking if I could join them, so I stopped at my children's table to stall and say hello.

But my kids seemed to always know what I was really doing.

"Just go over and sit by him!" they loudly said to me.

"Shhh," I reprimanded them, not wanting to be heard as they continued their playful nudging.

Finally, I walked over and asked if their group had room for one more. Jake warmly smiled at me and stood to pull out a chair.

As the reception commenced, so did the timeless comfort of reacquainted friends. We laughed until we had tears in our eyes as we joked and reminisced.

Soon the tables were cleared and the music began. The third song played was my favorite, "What a Wonderful World."

Now, completely enamored, I took Jake by the arm and led him to the floor.

"I just have to dance to this song," I boldly said to him.

But something happened that evening, I wasn't bound to forget.

Jake continued to ask me to dance in a myriad of ways. Each request felt more sincere than the one before.

"Does anyone want to dance?" he said, glancing my way.

"Anyone want to go out again?" he said, smiling at me.

"Shall we?" he asked softly as he reached out for my hand.

His invitations continued all night with complete regard for me. I hadn't known such kindness or reverence before.

And that night, while dancing with Jake, I remembered 'true love' again.

True love is pure sentiment directly from the heart, openly given and received with authentic and timeless affection.

There's nothing else in the mix.

True love is never taken.

Then a wave of sadness washed through me as I realized, I'd taken that first dance from Jake. I hadn't even asked him. I just led him to the floor. The catalyst had primarily been enamored self-indulgence.

And I thought of the countless couples who take from one another and boss each other around. They make 'honey-do-lists' for the other, not realizing how far from true love their actions unwittingly are.

But once again, Jake looked my way for yet another dance and I could see in his gentle eyes that all was completely forgiven.

As he took me by the hand and led me to the floor, I smiled with thanks for how profoundly he had changed my world.

Later at home, I was moved by the realization that my understanding of love had been backwards all along.

No wonder I found little happiness in it.

How extraordinary that it took someone from a previous life to help me remember the true love that was once inherent on Earth.

The next morning, I smiled as thoughts of Jake returned. I was fascinated by the opportunity to compare different versions of him based on my past life memories.

Most notable was his kindness that remained in various lives. How lucky I was to be aware of our timeless existence.

The following night, I awoke to find Jake's Higher Self by my bed. Under normal circumstances, if I awoke to find a man lurking in the dark, I'd totally be freaked out. But the spirit world isn't freaky at all, in fact, it's completely neutral.

Love is a neutral energy and the only vibration of which the higher realms are comprised.

When someone sees through intuitive eyes, they are seeing as spirit on Earth. And this is the neutral perspective of our Higher Selves.

In fact, everyone's essence is inherently neutral here. This is our true and transcendent state; we are infinite consciousness. The varied vibrations of human emotions are just on the physical plane.

Jake stood next to me smiling. He was happy we'd found one another again and my presence was flooded with absolute joy from our gentle communication.

As time went on, Jake's divine essence steadfastly remained with me. He had arrived, energetically, the week before the wedding.

* * *

As I stood in the kitchen one day, I thought of the 'real' Jake. There had been no word from him, since the day of the wedding.

"Jake's going through a pretty rough time and has a lot of healing to do," his ethereal presence explained.

I was disappointed, so he tried to soften the news.

"He thinks of you, but doesn't know why," he said with a casual shrug.

So I asked if we'd get together again in this present life.

"Don't you remember our contract?" he asked.

"You mean we agreed on a plan?" I thought as my Higher Self stepped in with a little more detail than that.

"We form contracts with one another before we are born on Earth. We set up the lessons and healing we want to accomplish while here. You and Jake made a contract to be together again, once you'd healed certain lessons," my Higher Self explained.

"You would each suffer pain and loss, then learn to trust again. Once this was accomplished, you would find one another and live in the love you have shared countless times before."

"So it's like one of those spiritual contracts on Oprah?" I slowly surmised.

"Not exactly, but you've got the idea." my Higher Self replied.

* * *

I was being led to the next phase in my life, but it felt more like a forced march. I was completely resistant to it, familiarity was more my style.

It was a process of out with the old and in with the new, and especially, on the spiritual plane, that means everything goes.

So no matter how hard I tried, my investment portfolio faded away, along with my ego and dreams, until nothing remained. And as beneficial as that may sound, it wasn't any fun.

"This is a lesson in absolute faith," my Higher Self often reminded me.

"Yup... and it totally sucks," I responded frequently.

* * *

When I first met Marina, I was completely dependent on her exceptional clarity. But as I healed, I began to see the visions around us as well and hear my own divine essence (Higher Self) speaking to both of us.

One day, Marina tuned into me and heard the following, "You've healed in a month, what takes most people several years to heal. Soon you will be transitioning to the fifth dimension, along with other advanced souls."

Marina looked at me to make sure I understood.

"Some souls are moving to a much higher frequency. You must be one of them," she explained. "The fifth dimension is where we are fully conscious of our intuitive powers and use them deliberately."

As Marina continued listening to my Higher Self, it became unclear, whether or not, I should keep my Sanibel home.

"It's a matter of choice now," my Higher Self explained. "You've finished healing the karma, your connection to the island has served. You've also received the gifts from the island to help you with your purpose. You can keep your home or let it go, either way is fine."

"I'm not quite ready to let it go," I responded to this. "It's criminal how they rip people off. Someone has to fight them."

"And just for the record, I'd like to know what karma really is," I asked. "Did I do something terribly wrong to somehow deserve all of this? Is it really an eye for an eye and a tooth for a tooth as some religions suggest?"

"Not at all," my Higher Self explained from within my consciousness. "The concept of karma, like many ideas, is greatly misunderstood. Its meaning has been twisted by leaders to serve a purpose for them."

"Karma is simply another chance, we each create for ourselves to neutralize unresolved energies and regain our balance in life. The higher realms are always supportive and have our best interests at heart. They are never punitive - that is misinformation."

Then I asked about the agreement, I apparently had with Jake.

"It's a divine contract between two souls and not a freewill choice," Marina explained. "It means you will be together again, when the time is right."

Marina noticed an energy cord of creative, magical energy coming into my second chakra to align me with my higher purpose in this present life.

I was also letting go of old-fashioned belief systems stored in my first chakra, regarding survival on Earth. Slowly, I was transforming into my optimal self and someday soon, I would be free to speak my truth in the world.

My economic demise was explained as the breakdown of my brain-based perspective in the physical world. This would open my consciousness to my inherent frequencies attuned to my optimal self.

Jake was clearly seen aligned with my heart chakra now.

All hopelessness in my solar plexus was on its way out. Buoyant energies of optimism and confidence were on their way in. And my eyes were in transformation, they were shifting to view myself as divine consciousness here.

We are all magical beings on a magical journey through life.

"Ask your guides to set up optimal scenarios of abundance for you," Marina suggested. "Your entire energy field is filled with a sparkling frequency that's enabling you to heal at a very fast rate!"

Later that week, I asked my guides to clear the blocks to my faith.

"It isn't time yet," they said.

"Could we at least clear some of them?" I persisted.

At once, I was in a vision in which the sky was filled with clouds as the sun burst forth with a deeper awareness that all creation is 'One.'

It was extremely cliché, and yet somehow, delightfully poignant.

A few days later, I tried to clear the blocks to my faith again. But they still wouldn't budge, so I focused on clearing more blocks to clarity instead.

Later, I sat in the stillness of the healing I had done as the Buddha appeared by my side.

"Padmasundara," he said to me as I remembered my name.

I was called, 'Beautiful Lotus' and smiled as the memories of that lifetime flooded my consciousness.

"Remember the middle path, dear one," he said. "Neutrality is inherent in all existence on Earth."

As I contemplated this notion, a universal compassion arose from the depths of my consciousness and I began to chant as the Buddha once chanted himself.

"May I attain enlightenment for the benefit of all creation," echoed throughout my form.

For hours, I sat in the stillness and for hours, I chanted the words.

As the day passed, the sun gently set and the night slowly deepened, so did the compassion within my awakening soul.

And through my dedication to the healing of all living things, I saw through the eyes of the Buddha within my very own.

Tears came with this new awareness.

Silence followed again.

"Now am I ready for absolute faith?" I asked my guides once more.

"You are," they confirmed as my faith disappeared and in its place, arose from within, a new level of clarity.

Chapter Three

The Chief

A week later, I was having a rotten day.

I had completed a new phase of healing that enabled me to upgrade my energetic circuitry to hold a much higher frequency, thereby bringing more of my own divine essence into my physical form.

The process included releasing old energetic patterns that were no longer helpful for me.

As the layers of unpleasant programming cleared from deep within, a stream of painful thoughts and feelings exited my system. I felt each emotion, acutely. It was no picnic that day.

During my meditation the following morning, I found myself in a powerful vision within my expanding awareness. A bonfire blazed on the beach, where our village had gathered that night.

Jake and I, along with our children (one was my daughter today), danced around the brilliant fire.

As if in flight through the heavens, we wore ceremonial wings as a native drum pulsed in the darkness and I heard the ancestors speak.

"Times of great upheaval are when the seeds of a much better future are more easily sewn in the present."

* * *

During my next visit with Marina, I asked if the physical Jake had feelings for me yet. Energetically, he was visibly with me all the time now.

"No, he's just with you for healing," Marina confirmed. "You're not fully with him either. The physical world is a very slow vibe. This may take some time."

In my next ethereal experience, I went back to the spiritual plane. I left my personality behind, having no cares or emotions.

I had no thoughts.

I was simply pure light.

I was infinite consciousness.

In silence, I stood on a beach. I wore a gauzy, white dress. The waves gently washed over my feet and buried my toes in the sand.

This was my sacred place on Earth, where I was my authentic self. I was on Sanibel Island.

"I know you can do this," Jake assured as he stood boldly beside me. "You must have faith in your purpose on Earth and things will go your way. You can't give up on becoming, who you are meant to be."

Then upon hearing the laughter of children, I looked toward my island home. I saw myself in the future, living a joyful life of abundance with grandchildren all around.

"How did I get there?" I asked my guides.

"Diligence," they confirmed.

* * *

A month later, I flew to Los Angeles to visit my daughter, who was in her first year of college there. A young woman sat next to me on the plane, who was spending a week in L.A. with her mom. It was a flight to remember.

At twenty years old, Tara was a medical wonder. She had beaten a fatal disease, contracted in her youth. When I asked, how she healed herself, she told me about the various forms of energy work she had done.

"Qigong, intuitive healing and other holistic methods completely saved my life," she said.

Tara was an exceptional soul. She had remembered her first past lifetime, when she was six years old. She was her own maternal grandmother, who lived before she was born.

And as our conversation continued, she shared many happy memories of other past lives she recalled.

I was both surprised and delighted to meet someone with past life memories not unlike my own. Feeling at ease, I told her about my life on the northern plains.

I described the nomadic village in which I peacefully lived and the day a band of warring braves rode suddenly from the woods.

Instantly, Tara looked at me with astonishment in her eyes, then stepped in to finish my narrative in which I lay in the sweet autumn grass as my little son and daughter were struck beyond my reach.

I looked at Tara in disbelief as she described every detail of our village being destroyed. And as she spoke a portal appeared in which we were also together in a very different life.

Tara was chanting to the heavens, until it was her time to die.

"I was the medicine woman in our village," Tara quietly said. "I sang the cross-over blessing, while everything burned to the ground. I was the last to go."

"You're serious..." I responded in total disbelief as we watched the scene unfold.

Then I looked directly at Tara as if trying to wake from a dream.

"I know," Tara acknowledged. "This is really weird. I guess, we were meant to sit together."

And soon, our plane touched down in L.A. and pulled into the gate. We gathered our bags as we departed and hugged one another goodbye.

* * *

As part of Higher Consciousness Training, I was attuned to practice Usui Reiki. This unique form of Japanese energy work is widely recognized as beneficial for physical and mental disease.

The founder of this method, Mikao Usui, was a direct descendent of the Hatamoto Samurai and a lifelong student of medicine, who maintained a high-vibrational spiritual practice throughout his life.

In 1922, he climbed Mount Kurama for a 21 day meditation and fast. There, he was shown a healing technique that doesn't deplete the healer, energetically.

I was intrigued, so I signed up for the Reiki course the next week.

As I walked into the sunlit room, I paused to take a breath as wisps of Reiki energy sparkled above each practitioner's head. I was drawn, inexplicably, to the delicate light.

As if by magic, it appeared from an invisible source, then flowed into each practitioner's crown and gently out through their hands.

Miraculously, it made luminous, any imbalance that needed to heal, as the smart energy seemed to independently do its ethereal work.

I asked the class to help clear my blocks to living abundantly. As they began working on me, it was clear I was out of whack.

I had healed so many survival issues, both collective and my own, that my first chakra (regarding survival on Earth) was greatly enlarged and in overdrive; it was squeezing out my second.

Our instructor, stepped in to correct the gross disparity and once the Reiki completed its work, I felt a dramatic shift take place as my chakras realigned.

Could this imbalance have been connected to my financial ruin?

At home, I felt immense relief with my chakras healthy again and hoped this change would bring financial abundance back into my life.

As I wondered, how I would get there, a telling past life came to light.

I was a newspaper man, who began as a copy boy. After a decade or so, I became a columnist. By my late fifties, I had authored several well-received books.

"This is your path to abundance," I heard a voice from within.

"What? I rarely read these days. How could I ever write?" my monkey-mind chattered at me.

The next day, I went back to class for my final Reiki attunement and certification protocol. Each of us would run Reiki energy into a fellow student, so Emily could check our abilities as practitioners.

I did my final assessment on Mary, a nurse who'd been practicing 'healing touch' on patients for many years.

As I began, the Reiki flowed where Mary needed to heal, with a surge of light, the divine energies filled our ethereal forms. And with this, I felt truly in concert with the universe.

After our graduation, Emily told me about a Reiki practitioner she had recently met.

"He's the best psychic surgeon I've ever seen. I watched him clear a woman of pancreatic cancer in less than an hour. It was incredible," she said. "He's a chief and medicine man, who lives in Florida. Maybe he could help you with your home on Sanibel Island."

When I got home, I was curious to learn more about the chief. His bio and contact information came up in the search results. So I sent him an email and asked if he could help fix the problems regarding my Sanibel home.

The chief wrote back at once.

"I have everything you need," he replied. "But you'll need to come to Florida and meet with me in person."

His response triggered waves of emotion that caught me by surprise as tears and cellular memory flooded my earthly presence.

Shortly thereafter, came pure relief in their enormous wake, so I gathered myself to respond.

"Perhaps, I can fly down next month as finances permit," I wrote back.

"You have to come down much sooner than that, next month will be too late," he responded.

Within hours, I booked a flight with air-miles that came from out of the blue and began packing a carry-on bag for a trip in just a few days.

"My wife and I invite you to stay at our home," the chief wrote again.

I accepted their invitation.

That night, a change occurred in me, far greater than when I met Jake. Jake was with me ethereally and providing constant support, but upon first contact with the chief, a much more dramatic shift began, along with a splitting headache.

It felt like a swelling balloon in my brain that was causing enormous pressure and pain as if my head would explode. The condition persisted for days.

When I viewed the shift clairvoyantly, it seemed my pineal gland and occipital region, through which we enter and exit the body as spirit, were in major decalcification-mode and coming back to life. The intense speed of this transformation was causing the pressure and pain.

The shift included new energy channels opening in my ethereal form with a distinct "snap, crackle, pop" as if

I'd poured milk on Rice Krispies, somewhere inside my brain.

Many parts of my original self had been dormant for thousands of years and were now expanding to embody more of my infinite consciousness within my physical form. I tried giving into the process, but my headache wouldn't subside.

Jake stood in the kitchen one night and smiled with sympathy.

"Can I help?" he asked in a gentle tone.

"That would be great," I replied.

He placed his hand on the back of my head and the other around my waist. With his support, I completely relaxed and fully gave into the pain, which released all resistance to change.

Instantly, my headache was gone and my transformation complete.

"How did you do that?" I asked with surprise as a much higher vibration flooded my human form.

Jake simply smiled.

And as we stood in the kitchen that night, our mutual love and support for each other filled us with heavenly light.

Jake was a powerful healer.

I had taken a quantum leap.

I noted the sound of my elegant pulse and was thankful to be alive.

* * *

I was beginning to see my life as a series of miracles.

Drawn to the chief with such swiftness, I wondered, if there was more to the story than I realized. So I sat down in a quiet place, took a deep breath and turned within as I tuned into our connection.

As I passed through a portal to collective memory, I found myself on a beach. I was a girl, about eighteen months old, an aboriginal child.

I looked over the sparkling ocean and up at the clear, blue sky. I sat in the sand as my short, little legs barely stretched beyond my small frock. It felt like my first time on Earth and I was on Sanibel Island.

My earthly manifestation was present in every regard.

I had strikingly clear and complex consciousness for such a young child. My plump, little toes wiggled with joy as I played in the warm, island sand.

A young man came by, who swept me up into his powerful arms. He carried me on his slender hip as I happily grabbed on.

"Cool," I thought as I recognized him, the chief was once my dad.

The planet was newly seeded, humanity lived in utopian times. Contentedly, I clung to his side as he walked and talked to the villagers on his daily rounds as our medicine man.

He vigilantly watched over me and protected me from harm. I was adored beyond measure, which left my consciousness pure and unscathed.

I had no karmic buildup, weighing my psyche down. I was simply pure spirit, animating a physical form.

The summer before, I remembered true love, while dancing in Jake's arms. Now, I realized wholeness-of-being in the powerful arms of my dad.

Words of love, honor and goodness were all I had ever known.

As I fast-forwarded the vision to my fourteenth year, I remained pure in consciousness and void of any doubt regarding my perfect presence on Earth.

Humanity was in balance. There were no gender roles. Both parents watched over their children and protected them from harm.

There were no forms of aggression nor systems of dominance. Everyone simply regarded themselves as portals of consciousness.

All people lived in a world comprised of the countless aspects of love. And with my new awareness, the powerful force of divine consciousness flooded my present day psyche.

* * *

My next visit with Marina sent me skyrocketing to a new level of growth and awareness. Marina began with a blessing, then tuned into my energy field.

Beside me, appeared a plain-looking man in a dark suit. He wore his hair in side curls and a yarmulke on his head. He was a striking departure from Jake's familiar presence.

"Who's that?" I asked, not recognizing this new energetic form, suddenly missing Jake and wondering where he had gone.

"He was your husband," Marina interpreted. "He's bringing in an element of Jewish mysticism for you. This will serve as a healing modality in your present life."

"And he's here to give you a message, but he's speaking far too softly for me to understand."

So Marina leaned in a bit closer, then finally sat back.

"I can't hear him," she confessed, then paused to try again.

"He seems to want to give the message directly to you," she said.

"But I'm not very good at this stuff," I responded hesitantly.

So, Marina asked for more information regarding why he'd appeared.

He explained, he hadn't crossed over from the lifetime

we would be shown. He was waiting to give me a message.

Once given, this past life aspect (his personality in that particular life) would rejoin his greater soul.

"But I don't have your clarity, Marina," I stalled uncomfortably.

"He wants to tell you directly. I don't know why," she explained. "I just know that he's waited a very long time to tell you something important and it may be worth while to listen."

So Marina asked to be shown the life in which he still remained as a vision appeared in which I had drowned, trying to save our son.

We were spending a day by the lake. Our little boy (my oldest today) played along the shore. Suddenly, he was out of sight.

We scanned the empty beach and began to fear the worst. Frantically, I dove into the water and drowned myself instead.

Not long after, our son was found further down the beach. And that was how I had tragically died, when I was his wife.

Again, the stranger offered the message he'd waited so long to tell as I looked at Marina with a silent cry for help.

"Just do your best," she encouraged. "Maybe you'll hear what he says.

So I gave into the stranger as he leaned closer in and softly spoke to me.

"You do not need to take responsibility for others. It isn't your job," he said. "Only they can save themselves."

Then he paused for a moment to let his words sink in.

"You need to release your subconscious belief that you should forfeit your life for others. You are not a sacrificial lamb. Nor are you a beast of burden for anyone in the world."

The poignancy of his message caught me by surprise, jogging my memory.

"You are equal to everyone," he emphasized to me. "By placing yourself first in life, you can surely help many more."

And with his heartfelt message, a gentle catharsis began.

"He's right," I said to Marina. "I've never valued myself as much as I've valued everyone else."

A moment later, he knew, his message had been received.

"He's ready to cross over," Marina said as a portal of light opened next to him. "Why don't you ask if there's anything else, he wants to say to you."

So, I finally opened my heart to the stranger in front of me.

Gently, he touched my cheek.

"I love you," he said with devotion. "I will always be grateful to you. I am deeply honored that you were once my wife."

His voice was so pure and tender, it caught me by surprise. Familiar feelings began to stir. I was sad to say goodbye.

"Do you know who that was?" Marina asked as I shook my head in response.

"Quickly, before he goes into the light, look into his eyes," she urged.

And in that final moment as he turned to glance my way, instantly, I recognized him; he was an aspect of Jake.

His tall silhouette gently faded as the portal began to close and from the last little twinkle of light, poured dozens of luminous roses as a final demonstration of his powerful love for me.

I sat transfixed, showered in light and wept unrestrainedly.

"How could I deserve such powerful love?" I wondered to myself.

"He honored you, so profoundly, because that's the kind of woman you are," Marina acknowledged my thoughts. "You deserve magnificent love and you will have it, I'm sure."

Slowly, Jake appeared in the room as his present day self again. He was visibly more complete, after regaining this past life aspect of his greater soul. And I looked into his infinite eyes with an ever expanding heart.

Then before I could take a breath, Marina saw something more; I was getting a 'Walk- In.'

Already emotionally spent, I looked at Marina blankly.

"A Walk-In is a whole new soul at a much higher frequency," she explained. "It's moving into your present day aspect as your new consciousness. There's a whole new you coming in!"

"In fact, it's entering through your second chakra as I'm telling you this. It's replacing the Higher Self that's been you on the earthly plane."

But this was a lot for me to handle in less than an hour's time.

"Your Walk-In has the heart-based connection important to your path," Marina explained. "This is a contractual exchange and not a matter of choice."

"You've agreed to have these new energies bring in a higher frequency, when the time is right. It will enable you to accomplish your life's purpose with much greater ease."

"You will still be you on many levels, but you can also expect some change."

Marina tried to comfort me as I turned noticeably pale.

"A more appropriate being now inhabits your presence on Earth, filled with the energies you will need to do what you came here to do. A Walk-In is a twin to the soul you have been so far and a very rare occurrence."

"Each of our souls have many facets that shift in and out of our energy fields as our life requires. But a Walk-In is not a simple facet exchange, it's a new and more aligned duplicate, taking the original soul's place," she explained.

So I watched the translucent mist of the being I would become enter through my second chakra as the soul exchange neared completion."

"And just as a massive earthquake can destroy all life upon it, so did I feel equally shaken by this experience. And when it was over, all things considered, I felt exceedingly numb.

Later at home, I stood in the kitchen making my afternoon tea. I was in awe of the beauty in life. I was humbled by the miracles.

I looked at the family photos adorning the front of my fridge. I was blessed to have such wonderful kids. They willingly loved and supported me, no matter how weird I was.

Then I remembered more about the past life I had seen. As Orthodox Jews, our lives were centered around the God of our faith.

Our rituals and traditions acknowledged God's divine essence in music, art, wisdom and love. We knew God is in all creation.

I also remembered my husband and every detail of him.

I was grateful for this aspect of Jake, who had loved me so profoundly that he'd stayed behind to deliver his cathartic message.

Because of his unconditional love, I was able to open my heart to loving myself again. And from this shift, ironically, came selfless love from deep within.

While cooking my dinner that evening, I pulled out the little breadboard next to the warm stove and sat on a cushioned stool.

Now that my kids were gone, this was my new tradition. It was far cozier there, than the dining room table alone.

Jake appeared as I ate my meal and my heart swelled with fondness for him.

"I don't think I've ever been loved so deeply and profoundly before," I thought.

"Are you God?" I blurted on reflex, surprised by my own words.

"Well, in a way, I guess, I am," he twinkled, joyfully.

"Of course, you are, and so am I," I echoed back at him.

And together, we laughed in the kitchen that night, feeling rather giddy.

* * *

The next morning, I awoke in a state of existential angst, grappling with the implications of yesterday's soul exchange.

I was lying on the floor of the chasm the concept had torn through my psyche that night. Panic had settled in. But eventually, I was able to articulate my concerns.

"What is a Walk-In anyway? Could such an occurrence erase the person I have always been? I don't really feel

that different, yet I wonder, am I gone?" I sorted
through the piles of refuse in my frazzled mind.

"Am I still here or somewhere else? Is the person my
thoughts are coming from someone other than me? If
so, then where am I? And why am I so freaked out about
someone I may no longer be?"

I jumped to my knees and looked at the oval mirror at
the head of my bed. At least I look the same, I thought,
as I laughed at my disheveled morning hair and
overloaded brain.

A bit calmer now, I noticed, the 'I' in my mind's chatter
had remained fully intact. There had been no alteration
to the 'I' with which I defined myself.

But I felt many subtle changes, like a centuries-old
sequoia with a much better vantage point, than the
sapling it had been.

I was shown, the 'I' of which we're comprised is not as
simple as the 'I' the human mind can grasp.

Our concept of self is also comprised of many different
soul aspects, soul facets and advanced, multidimensional
versions of our greater self that converge to form the
energy matrix (the substance of infinite consciousness)
through which we perceive our existence from many
unique dimensions at any given time.

Could this higher perspective be restored in our species
again?

"It's time to trust my own answers," I acknowledged that
day.

In my Native American lifetimes (based on my own memory), one consulted their ancestors, then followed their own unique voice. The next day, I would fly to Florida to meet the chief and his wife.

Chapter Four

The Heart

I was surprisingly calm as my plane touched down, but as I arrived at the West Melbourne home my brain started freaking out.

"Are you crazy, you don't even know these people," my monkey-mind chattered at me. "Seriously, are you nuts? Just turn and walk away. I'm telling you... get... back... into... the car!"

But my Higher Self outstretched my finger to ring the bell of the tropical home.

In a moment, the front door opened as the chief and his wife greeted me with smiles and welcoming hugs.

Instantly, I felt at ease.

As we sat at the kitchen table drinking fresh lemonade from the trees in the yard, the chief acknowledged my thoughts.

"I'm not what you expected," he bluntly remarked. "But I'm an indigenous chief. Unlike other North American tribes, we are of Caribbean descent."

"Oh," I responded awkwardly, unsettled by how easily he had read my questioning mind.

"Are you a Priestess or a Shaman?" the chief, then abruptly asked.

"Not that I know of," I answered, not sure what those things even were.

A look of mild disappointment crossed his gentle face as he talked about tribal traditions, their culture and history.

"We were the original humans with whom the planet was seeded," the chief began. "Throughout our history, we have always lived as a peaceful society."

"We know that 'being human' is to live one's life from the heart. It's about living as spirit in this spiritual world and to live as 'One' with 'The Great Spirit' - the creator of all that exists."

As he continued to speak, he referred to himself as a medicine man.

"What does a medicine man do?" I asked.

"He doesn't 'do' anything," the chief explained. "He 'is' the medicine."

"How does one become a medicine man?" I asked after that.

"You can't become a medicine man. It's just what you are," he said.

After his wife said goodnight, I spoke to the chief, candidly.

"When we connected online, I recalled an indigenous life," I began. "I remembered myself as a baby girl about eighteen months old and I knew it was my first time being human on Earth."

"I was sitting in the sand, when a young man came by, who picked me up and took me along with him. He was the medicine man in our village and he was my dad."

Then I turned to directly face the chief and looked into his eyes.

"I know, my dad was you," I announced with masked trepidation.

"We wondered if you would ever talk," responded the chief knowingly, as he looked, for the first time in a very long time, into his daughter's eyes.

The double entendre sent waves of shock throughout my consciousness as I held his glance for just a moment and tears ran down my cheeks.

Then I lowered my eyes from his, overwhelmed that he also knew me.

Before getting up to say goodnight, the chief explained something more.

"Tomorrow you will go back through the portal from which you came into this world, so you can become fully human again. The angel who brings us here at birth will be acting as your guide. You will regain full consciousness."

"When we're connected to The Great Spirit, we're given all we need; love, joy and abundance."

Then, the chief leaned closer in.

He looked deeply into my eyes.

"You are one of the chosen," he said in a weighty tone.

"The world is filled with many men, but you are one, who will be noted in the history of humankind."

"Humanity has lost consciousness as a species on Earth, but you didn't lose your divine connection when you came into this world. You are extremely rare."

As I sat in silence, trying to fathom his words, my brain began shouting inside my head, "Now you're totally freaking me out!"

The chief smiled with compassion and said, "Enough, it's time for bed."

The next morning, we went out for breakfast. The chief spoke of many things. He talked about humanity's unconscious state and lack of connectivity.

"When we first walked the planet, we were each in the image of the divine," he began. "This is the clarity you possessed, when I was your dad."

"We consciously used our clairvoyance and healing abilities. Spoken language was unnecessary. Our telepathic communication was far more complex and well-suited to the complexity of divine mind."

"Even though we've lost these skills on many levels today, divinity remains inherent in everyone of us. It simply lies dormant in the unconscious mind," he explained.

"But the world is on the brink of reawakening. Soon, we will live our lives as divine presence again."

As we walked on the beach after breakfast, the chief commented, thoughtfully.

"I've noticed you talk about people loving you, but I haven't heard you use the words 'I love' in our conversations yet."

I was completely caught off guard by his observation; it was one, I hadn't made myself. I looked at the ground self-consciously, suddenly aware of the state of 'wanting' in which I had always been, realizing how little I truly loved, consumed by the need to receive it instead.

But then, with his medicine guiding me, I looked back into his eyes as a profound shift took place somewhere deep inside me.

Now, in my heart to infinite depths, my awareness settled in as I transitioned from looking for love to someone simply giving it.

"Being fully self-actualized is to live in love," the chief explained. "In the beginning, we lived from the heart and gave from the heart, but we never gave it away. It is the sacred place from which we live and love as humans."

"Today, when we fully live from the heart, we remind others to do the same."

With this shift in perspective and my transformation complete, I opened my heart, as in the beginning, and consciously settled in.

"Now you have made the journey, you came here to make," he confirmed. "The journey from the head to the heart is the sacred bridge within."

"Crossing this ethereal bridge is essential to 'being human' and fully self-actualized. This is where you will now reside for the rest of your time in the world."

As we continued our morning walk, the chief gentle asked, "Do you have a man?"

A bit embarrassed, I shook my head.

"I have two puppies, who keep me company," I answered.

"You should have someone," he persisted in a fatherly tone, then after a thoughtful pause, he tried again.

"Is there anyone who interests you?" he asked.

"Kind of..." I said. "His name is Jake."

"Does he call you?" he asked.

"Not at all," I shrugged.

"Hmph!" the chief loudly protested. "He still doesn't speak much!"

"Let's walk down to the shore," he suggested.

As we approached the water's edge, we slipped out of our shoes. We let the cool ocean waves bury our feet in the sand.

"Look straight out at the water and tell me what you see," the chief said.

"Now that we've stepped into the waves, the water is all I can see," I said.

"Very good," he said, then spoke metaphorically.

"When we look in one direction, we limit our point of view. If the mind can only see water, we think it is all that exists."

"For many in this condition, the world is like being lost at sea. And this is the current condition of most of humanity."

"Now tell me, what do you 'know' apart from the view?" he asked.

"I know, we've just stepped into the waves and we're only ankle-deep," I said. "Even though I can't see the shore, I know we're still standing on land."

"Very good," the chief responded, smiling at me. "But the unconscious human condition has no awareness of this. They don't know where we've come from or where we still stand."

Then, he looked directly at me as I looked over at him.

With the slightest shift in perspective, we could both see the shore again.

"Even for those unconscious, 'seeing' is easily regained. We must simply learn to view the world in a more expansive way."

"As the shore extends into the water and the waves wash over the land, so it is with heaven and Earth," the divine instructor said. "The physical world and the spiritual world are really one and the same."

I looked at the chief, quizzically.

"You're almost there," he said.

"It's such a magical world," I thought as we continued our walk.

"It's not a 'magical' world," said the chief, reading my mind again. "It's a spiritual world with spiritual people. All of us are of 'The Great Spirit' and all of the world is the same. Everything, including us, is spiritual energy."

Later that day, all too quickly, our time had come to an end. As he walked me to my car, I was filled with admiration.

"Thanks for your support and guidance," I sincerely said. "You sure must have a large following, you're such an incredible teacher."

"I am not anyone special and I have no following," the chief responded. "I am simply human, just like everyone else."

"But you know, what I mean," I persisted.

"No, I don't," he held his ground. "If someone tries to follow me, I turn and look them straight in the eye, and tell them to follow themselves!"

"We each have our own unique path in the world and mine is for me alone. You're never the best you can possibly be, when you're following somebody else."

"Your house will be fine now," he confirmed. "And soon you will be awake. You've made the journey you came here to make into the sacred heart and you must remember, you alone, create your destiny."

Then he paused for my fullest attention and spoke instructively.

"When you wish for something, don't envision an end result. You will only restrict the outcome with the limits of your mind. Just hand it off and let it go. Be patient and steadfast within."

"Never let go of your faith in your vision - the physical world is slow. Always align with your inner truth. Spirit answers every prayer."

"You must realize an absolute truth; all existence is divine and all is divine creation."

"Thank you," I said, now ready to go. "I love you!"

"I love you too," he said with a hug.

Our time had come to an end.

* * *

I met with Marina the following week. As I talked about my trip, the chief's ethereal presence appeared directly behind me.

"The chief is a powerful support for you," Marina said about this.

I had gone through many changes over the past two weeks. I was corded to a bright, orange fireball at my third chakra, greatly increasing my power on the physical plane.

And my Walk-In was bringing life-purpose energy in through my fifth chakra as quickly as my body could handle it.

Marina looked a bit closer and was puzzled by the energies of my new soul. It seemed, my new Walk-In hadn't been to this planet before.

"Are you an inter-dimensional mix of divine races?" Marina asked. "For example, are you Galactic (a being from multiple galaxies), Arcturian (an advanced vibrational architect) or perhaps an Evolved One (an Ascended Master)? Are you any of those?"

"I'm a little of each," my Walk-In replied. "But most of my energies come from a higher dimensional abstraction called, 'The Utopia of Unification.'"

Marina hadn't heard of this, so she did her best to explain my new soul's origin.

"It's difficult to describe where your Walk-In is from," she said. "It's a very high vibration and hasn't been to this planet since spoken language began."

"The closest descriptor we have is 'Unity,' but that's not exactly it. Realistically, you are comprised of energies we have no words to describe."

"You'll be going through many changes now. Your system will be moving to a much higher frequency than ever before as the embodiment of unification essential to your path. You're downloading all you will need, along with a lot more."

As the download began, I thought of my first human life, when the chief was my dad. Earth was a utopia, when humans first seeded the planet. We instinctively knew that all existence combines to create the energy matrix, we call, 'the physical world.'

Humans consciously interacted with love, respect and reverence as integral presence in nature. This was how aware we were of our unified consciousness. We knew all existence is One.

Marina could hear my thoughts as they were coming to mind.

"Your life's purpose is to help other people realize this as well," she interpreted. "This is your optimal path."

When I returned home, I sat down to meditate. I thought of my time in Florida and the chief's meditation practice and wondered if his techniques were different from my own.

Mid-thought, he started sending the answer into my energy field as my frequency took a quantum leap to what felt like a new stratosphere.

Rather than running energies separate from myself, I felt the cosmos in its completeness arise from the depths of my soul.

"We don't have to connect to the earth, the cosmos or The Great Spirit," the chief explained. "We are not separate from them."

"The universe and beyond is in every cell of existence. We remain the divine Creators of our reality, while having a human experience."

"Is there anything else I should know?" I asked.

"Allow yourself to give into it and you will see," he said.

So I let go of all expectations and let myself fully give in as a self-sustaining completeness arose from the depths of my infinite soul of everyone and everything in the cosmos and beyond, each unique presence indistinguishable from the other.

* * *

I was focused on meditation more than ever now.

I saw Marina the following week and we talked about our news.

Jake popped into the room as I finished my narrative.

An energy cord with a 'witness' appeared between the two of us, so I asked what a witness was.

"It's symbolic imagery," Marina interpreted. "In this case, it symbolizes the residue from the past lifetimes you and Jake have shared."

"Lower vibrations from previous lives can weigh our psyches down. But it looks as though you and Jake are ready to clear yours' away."

So we cleared our past life lessons until the witness was gone.

Jake gently helped me unravel the past life debris that was binding my heart. Like unwinding a ball of ethereal twine, he slowly untangled the layers of pain, fear and uncertainty constricting my fourth chakra and causing resistance to love.

Soon, my heart was fully released and I did the same for him. Now, the lessons we once created were fully neutralized. Our abilities to love would no longer have limitations.

The chief came into the room with a peace pipe in his hands. It symbolized using one's unique voice as a positive force in the world and he wanted to pass it on.

Abruptly, I looked at Marina with panic in my eyes.

"Are you serious?" my monkey-mind chattered loudly inside my brain. "I can barely take care of myself. How could I help anyone?"

Both of them smiled at my reaction and waited for me to calm down

"Whatever you say," I thought to myself. "This should be interesting."

"Enough!" the great chief thundered. "You have to have faith in your path. You have to trust the process you're in and fully believe in yourself."

That night as I made my dinner, the chief appeared again.

"You need to get going on your life," he advised his little fledgling.

"But I thought you said, 'The Great Spirit provides everything we need,'" I recited.

"That's right," he confirmed. "The Great Spirit sends whatever we need, in addition to each of us doing our best."

"So… I do my best and God does the rest," I jingled back at him.

Before bed, I thought of how lazy I'd been, discouraged and tired, just wanting to rest. At times, I missed the good old days, when life was completely 'normal' without all of this spiritual stuff.

"Alright, I'm getting off my ass and doing my best with my life," I announced to myself in the kitchen that night and unwittingly to my guides.

I hadn't heard from Jake since the wedding, despite his ethereal presence being with me all along. I wished he could see the things I saw, so he could enjoy my support.

Then I thought it might be nice to send him a card to wish him well.

So I sat down and began to write, "Dear Jake..." when his ethereal presence looked over my shoulder with curiosity.

"I'm writing to tell your present day self how special you are to me," I explained as we smiled at the irony.

"How do you think he will take it?" I asked.

"It will certainly stir things up," he said.

"But will it help him heal?" I asked.

"Absolutely!" he answered, robustly. "And once the dust settles, it will kick my earthly presence into high gear!"

"Can you help me write it, so it has the best impact?" I asked.

He responded affirmatively.

So Jake's energetic presence dictated a letter to himself as I wrote it down. And here's what it said…

"Dear Jake, If I could change one thing in my life, I would have said, "Yes" the night you asked, "What would you say, if I asked you to marry me?" because that is the timeless answer I have always held in my heart…"

"Is that it?" I asked my coauthor.

"Yup," he replied with a grin as I began to wonder, if this was a good idea.

"Absolutely," he insisted. "It will scare him at first, but that's what he needs, something to jolt him out of his stupor and back to life again."

"Should I send it?" I asked.

"Indeed!" he declared.

Later that day, the card was in the mail.

Jake appeared the next morning with a mischievous look on his face.

"What are you beaming about?" I asked, especially charmed by him.

"The card," he said as his eyes lit up. "It will totally freak him out!"

"I know..." I worried, then realized, "That's exactly why we sent it!"

The next week, the 'real' Jake got the card.

How did I know?

I was sitting in my living room, when his ethereal image appeared in a giant wave of emotion. Jake was holding his face in his hands, sobbing dramatically.

And I noted, the image of Jake before me was not his Higher Self (the neutral presence I was used to seeing everyday), but instead, the embodiment of his emotions was sitting in front of me, along with a flood of past life debris.

I watched with fascination as oceans of pain, fear and sadness poured from his energy field. He was in shock and unable to speak.

I felt compassion for him, but decided to let him be.

"Are you okay?" I asked, later in the day.

"I'm just in shock," he responded. "I need some time to cry."

As I sat quietly next to him, my affection only grew.

"My goodness, I love this man," I thought.

"I know," he whispered back.

Three days later, the kids were home. It was Christmas Eve. Jake was doing better. He had cried himself out the first day and slept through the next.

Being loved unconditionally was a total shock for him.

The neutrality of my energy field was the perfect place to be, so I vigilantly watched over him as he slept through another day, allowing himself to heal.

On the fourth day, I awoke to find Jake standing next to my bed.

"Merry Christmas!" he said with extra cheer.

He was in a wonderful place.

My heart warmed upon seeing him finished with his enormous release and it seemed the time was growing near when I'd actually 'be' with him.

* * *

Two weeks later, I went to Marina's for a cup of tea. Within minutes, Jake came forward in my energy field.

"You need to claim your land on Sanibel," he announced. "By bringing your relationship with the earth into balance again, you will help humanity heal its relationship with the planet as well."

I was shown the vast amount of suffering held by the land. Like a cancer on her surface, it was cutting off interconnectedness and creating disharmony.

As energy cords from the two of us ran deeply into the earth, we smiled at one another as our aboriginal facets came forth.

"Two or more souls are required to accomplish this task," the higher realms explained. "Because you have cleared your past residue, your combined vibration is high enough to begin clearing human debris from the earth as well."

A third cord appeared between us that held another witness as we cleared the symbolic imagery with Marina's support.

Slowly, the witness started to shrink as the planet's vibration increased, then a mist arose from her surface as she became luminous.

This would be one of many steps in healing the sacred Earth.

As the witness faded away into a twinkle of light, we noticed a rainbow of images projecting from where it had been.

We stared in amazement as each little twinkle held a vision of the lives Jake and I had shared. As we focused on each living portal, every last detail was there.

"How could we have had so many lifetimes together?" I said of the magical sight. "There must be hundreds of them!"

"I know, it's really amazing!" Marina could see them as well. "But you were among the original souls, who first seeded the planet, so you've been here a very long time. The higher realms have sent this gift to thank you for helping the world."

And on that day, I aligned with 'Source' (Creation) and my 'True Self' (Divinity), then Marina asked me to picture my consciousness as a precious gem.

"Now place the gem inside of your heart," she gently said to me.

As I did, the gem burst into a fire deep within my soul.

Instantly, I turned into my aboriginal facet once more.

Now on the spiritual plane, I stood hand in hand with others, who were drawn to the blazing light.

As those who first seeded the planet, we were nonresistant to the path we had chosen on Earth.

We knew this sphere of consciousness would become a fragmented realm and we would learn many lessons, apart from neutrality.

This was the path we had chosen to evolve as collective mind. Thus, we stepped into the fire of our own divine creation.

Once we were gone, the flames arose into a circle of light, comprised of infinite visions portraying the evolution of life.

And just as the previous rainbow had been filled with our many past lives, so was this cycle of evolution filled with every detail of our journey into the mind, where human awareness slowly became a fractured paradigm.

Emotional frequencies lower than love were held in our energy fields, expanding human awareness beyond neutrality. And when our karmic buildup approached its absolute peak, great prophets were sent to the physical realm to end our suffering.

Many pure souls brought words of forgiveness and unconditional love, but very few people could hear what they said, through their own energetic fog.

As I processed the vast amount of information the vision held, I noticed a sparkling beam of light streaming into the world and knew, the higher forms of existence have come to intervene and bring humanity's evolution to swift and successful fruition.

And as I watched the fire burn down, from the final wisps of smoke, arose countless images taking shape as the ancients returning to Earth.

They are already here among us in many shapes and forms, gently helping us to remember who we really are.

"We are all beings of consciousness," the higher realms pointed out. "We are, by nature, nonphysical and we are the substance of Source."

Chapter Five

The Earth

Although I hadn't seen the 'real' Jake since the wedding, when I remembered true love while dancing in his arms, he continued to show his support for me, energetically.

I wanted to reciprocate with something he could fathom, so I decided to knit a prayer shawl for him.

I would make it with good intentions and blessings in every stitch. This would be my way of saying thank you and showing support.

I chose a yarn with the beautiful colors of a mountain stream and found bobbles to finish it 'fly-fisherman-style,' then began knitting the following week.

As I cast on with a déjà vu, tears came to my eyes and my heart swelled with the realization, I'd knit for him many times.

Humanity will someday remember the timelessness of love and this will surely be a wakeup call for everyone of us.

The beauty of the world is far beyond anything we can imagine.

* * *

The next week, I met with Marina for more insight into my healing. The residue between Jake and myself was gone ethereally, but could take a year or more to neutralize on a cellular level.

When it comes to physical change, too much too fast can make the body go into shock, it seems.

Marina helped me download a new relationship template to match who I am today.

"You may notice a shift in your friendships, once this assimilates," she explained. "Some people will disappear, if they no longer fit your path."

As my energy field transformed with the new template in place, Jake watched with fascination, so Marina offered a new one to him and he happily accepted.

A lot of healing can take place on one's own, but when two or more are gathered, a synergy often occurs that elevates the healing to a much higher frequency than can be achieved alone.

This was why Jake was hanging around, we were helping each other heal.

* * *

The next morning with coffee in hand, I sat down to meditate. It was my way of beginning each day, sipping my coffee and settling into a neutral and peaceful place.

As I gained more clarity, the infinite world of energy became more apparent to me. And with this, my ever expanding awareness had fewer collective constraints.

When we heal the many layers of our subconscious mind, the fractured pieces of our true presence always realign, until we regain the neutral perspective of that which we truly are; infinite consciousness.

That morning, I gazed at the clear, blue sky in neutral meditation and noticed the glow of the planet with its massive energy field.

And from this ethereal light came forth a strikingly elegant being, who stood in the morning sunlight streaming into my living room.

"You must be Mother Earth," I surmised.

"I am," the presence replied.

Her eyes sparkled brightly, as the glitter of reflecting light upon the ocean waves.

"What can I do for you?" I asked, not knowing what else to say.

"Tell them, I'm real," she requested. "Earth is divine presence just like everyone else. I am in the image of Source just like all creation. And I want to provide abundance for all, but humans no longer love. They take from me, rarely giving to me, until I have nothing left. Please help them remember true love again, before they destroy themselves."

"I promise, I'll let people know," I said.

In response, Mother Earth bowed her beautiful head and folded her hands in front of her heart as my ethereal presence arose and positioned itself in mirror image of her.

As we bowed our heads together, our divine awareness merged and from this union of consciousness I heard the following words…

"The human species is suffering. It's rife with imbalance, corruption and societal decay. Humanity must reawaken, before it is too late."

Then she raised her powerful glance to look at me once more and smiled like a confident parent as she gracefully faded away.

I remained in the stillness, trying to grasp our exchange.

"I need to tell people about this," I thought. "I never dreamed, she's a soul in a body just like everyone else."

Then I began to wonder, if I would sound totally crazy talking about this stuff and began to consider my options.

Perhaps, I could share my experience as a work of science fiction. That would make it more palatable as simple imagination, so people could shift their perspectives in their own unique time and way.

Countless leaps in science and culture have come from human imaginings.

"It's time to tell my story," I realized after that.

"People will think I'm nuts!" my monkey-mind chattered back.

"I'm okay with that," I shrugged.

* * *

My economic demise continued relentlessly.

The real estate market was crashing and no matter how hard I worked, my finances only grew worse. They had turned off my wifi at home and other amenities. I was unable to pay my bills.

"At least, the kids are away at college and I still have electricity," I tried to cheer myself up. "They can't turn that off in this frozen tundra, until it warms up in the spring."

I continued to knit every evening. Soon my gift for Jake had only two skeins to go.

I was honored to know him, if only in spirit, and prayed the care spun into my work would somehow be healing for him.

But as I sat there knitting, countless fears swirled around in my head.

"Be patient, my child," Mother Earth assured. "Everything will be fine."

Later, the chief came into the room and looked into my uneasy eyes.

"You're going to be alright, you know," he said, comfortingly.

"I know," I robotically answered, despite my worrying mind.

"No, you don't!" he roared at his unruly child.

"Okay, I'll figure it out," I whined.

The next day, I felt overwhelmed.

What was I supposed to write to turn my life around?

I was not cut out for this stuff!

Regardless, I gathered my journals and began flipping through them. I'd recorded my poignant experiences and conversations verbatim for more than twenty years.

Rereading them, I found my story hard to believe myself.

Yet, I knew with absolute certainty that my perceptions were 'real' as a window into the many layers of the subconscious mind, which determines the quality of our lives more than we can fathom.

Perhaps I could simply tell the truth.

Maybe that would suffice?

* * *

Later that week, I had lunch with Marina. Among many other things, I talked about writing a book.

"It could be about someone who recalls their past lifetimes and even the people in them," I began. "And how transcendent love really is from one lifetime to the next."

"This healing process has been so positive for me, although it may not suit everyone, perhaps, it could do some good."

After a pause, I commented, "It's such a beautiful love story, don't you think?"

"It is," responded Marina. "But there might be more to it than that."

* * *

Several days later, I found myself back in my Jewish lifetime again. I remembered our family outing, a picnic by the lake. I thought more about how I had drowned trying to save my son.

In a vision, my family stood before me on the ethereal plane. Jake had been my husband and Annie his sister back then. She helped him raise our little boy, after I was gone.

"I'm sorry, I left you so early and caused you so much pain," I said to both of them. "I hope you can forgive me."

"Of course, we forgive you," they assured. "We did a long time ago."

My little boy sweetly smiled at me as I lifted him onto my lap, then wrapped my arms around him and kissed him all over his head.

"I love you, I love you, I love you forever," I gratefully said to him.

Then, I turned to the past life aspect of my Higher Self (my personality in that particular life) and forgave myself for leaving my precious, loved ones behind.

And as I expressed these sentiments, a subconscious fear was released that I hurt the people I love the most, no matter how hard I try.

And with this release came a deeper fear to be neutralized as well, a fear that made me withholding toward the people I love the most in an effort to shield them from harm.

As my awareness came back to the present, I noticed a wonderful change, so I closed my eyes and took a deep breath, then tried something new.

"This is for all the people I have ever been," I announced to the universe. "I forgive myself, I forgive myself, I forgive myself, I forgive myself..." I repeated again and again.

As I chanted these powerful words of unconditional love, my ethereal form bowed her heavenly face into her hands and wept.

She wept more deeply than ever before with the grace of my own forgiveness and as she did, I released countless years of boundless guilt and pain.

I also let go of residual fears that can often accompany this and with each and every ethereal tear, I was filled with my own divine essence instead.

I saw Marina the following day.

Jake was there as usual next to my energy field as we continued to heal in tandem. I told her about the prayer shawl I was knitting for him.

"It would be beneficial to energetically merge his soul contracts with the shawl," she suggested. "The codes and vibrations he needs to heal could be placed in the yarn as well."

* * *

I was going through major paradigm shifts on all levels now. If someone had asked me years ago, if I believed in past lifetimes, I would have shrugged my shoulders with a 'whatever' response.

If someone had asked, if I was clairvoyant or could see energetically, I would have laughed politely and questioned their sanity.

And if someone had asked, if I could visit other times and places via energetic portals, I would have wondered where their straight jacket was.

In fact, I was healing so rapidly that my brain could barely keep up with my changes in perspective. And I knew, I was getting closer to 'truth,' whatever that really is.

The following week, I finished knitting the prayer shawl for Jake. I edged it with tassels from the same yarn, then added feathered, fly-fishing lures with iridescent glass fish. It was truly a gift from the heart.

Not long after, I saw Marina.

As she said a blessing and tuned into my energy field, a past life contract came to light deep in my second chakra. It was blocking my ability to move forward in my life.

Symbolic of a soul contract that had remained unfulfilled, I appeared stuck in a dark, deep hole, tightly gripping a piece of paper in my ethereal hands. The hole represented past trauma that had remained on a cellular level.

As we watched, a portal opened with another past lifetime to view. I had lived in Austria in the 17th century. My husband was once again Jake. We both laughed upon seeing him.

"Is he in every lifetime?" I asked.

"Not at all," said Marina, shaking her head. "We just see the lives that are useful for us. But I have to admit, I've never seen such consistency between two people before."

In the vision, I was holding the hand of our three-year-old son (my mother today). We were walking home in the early spring.

The sun was warm, though the air a bit chilly, the ground was still covered with snow. We followed the path from town through the woods, contentedly strolling home.

We were bundled in woolen winter wear, I had made for us by hand. My coat was tailored ankle length in a rich, charcoal gray. My son's attire was lighter in hue with embroidered accents on the collar, cuffs and hatband.

As we watched this past life unfold, a bear silently leapt from the woods. It struck me without warning. I was rendered instantly dead.

And in the same mighty swipe of its paw, my son was taken as well. It happened in less than an instant. The mother and child were gone.

As the portal continued, the only person who really suffered was Jake - he had died of a broken heart. And in doing so, he had crossed over, wanting to be with us.

But the bear's strike happened so quickly, as if in the absence of time, that our past life aspects remained transfixed in the earthly realm.

Mother and child remained hand-in-hand, walking in spirit only.

Marina spoke to this past life aspect of my greater soul and explained, she had died a long time ago.

"It's okay to cross over now," she said.

But the spirit gave no response, so Marina asked me to help.

As I merged my present day self with the woman I had once been, I shuddered from the numbing cold of her energetic void. And with our consciousness merged into one, I began to understand.

The trauma of her sudden death and inability to save her child had impacted her so profoundly that it shattered her psyche that day and short-circuited her ability to perceive reality.

Even with my present day self fully within her now, this past life aspect remained in a vacuum, oblivious to what had transpired.

"It's like she's completely frozen," I spoke from within her subconscious mind as fear, shock and confusion began to overwhelm me.

So Marina asked her loved ones, from that particular life, to help her walk into the light.

Jake and others appeared in a portal, gently coxing her toward them, but she remained unresponsive. Instead, she displayed profound grief and failure, regarding the death of her child.

Marina brought the tunnel of light directly to her face as the vast support of those she loved amplified the light.

Startling her, the light broke through and into her numbing void.

Slowly, she noticed, she wasn't walking home with her son that spring day.

Gradually, she realized, a great deal of time had gone by.

As Jake stepped from the portal, he put his arm around her and encouraged her to walk into the light, but she couldn't move and didn't know why. She just stood there helplessly.

So Marina asked Jake to carry her and he willingly obliged.

Securely, held in his loving arms, she transitioned into the light. And as she did, she let go of the past as their little boy walked beside them.

I asked, why their son hadn't crossed over, independently.

"He could have," Marina confirmed. "But he chose to stay with his mother and comfort her instead."

Then I thought about my past life, when I drowned trying to save my son. No wonder, I'd reacted extremely - the dynamic was amplified subconsciously by my past life inability to save my precious child.

And I thought of my Native American life on the northern plains. This was another time, I hadn't been able to save my children.

And it struck me as incredible that the human mind is so poignantly linked to our unresolved past.

* * *

The next day, I showed Marina the prayer shawl I had finished for Jake as a portal opened above us, where the 'Akashic Records' are kept.

We asked that the shawl be filled with the best of everything needed in life and watched as a stream of beautiful light poured into the heartfelt gift, including the optimal purpose that Jake would assimilate.

Once the download was complete, I reverently wrapped the gift with green and pink tissue paper, symbolic of healing and heart. Then I sealed it with wildflower stickers, sprinkled all over the top.

When finished, the package gently glowed from the heavenly light within it.

And I realized, all healing is self-healing, there isn't anything else.

When one receives help from another, such as my heartfelt gift, their Higher Self is always in charge and determines whatever transpires.

Others can help accelerate healing we choose to do for ourselves, but each of us knows best how to heal our unique presence on Earth.

I awoke at 4 A.M. to find the chief standing in my room.

"The kindness of the gift you sent Jake will provide the warmth he needs to melt his deepest fear and pain," he said. "His sacred heart will soon beat again with the pulse of divine existence."

A week later, I was working at home, when I felt a wave of unusual energy gently wash into the room.

I turned to see Jake, ever so quiet, wrapped in the prayer shawl I'd sent.

The next morning, his ethereal presence remained as it had been, wrapped within the shawl.

"Are you okay?" I asked as he gave a simple nod.

"I know who you are," he gently said. "You were once my wife."

"You're the one I've been looking for," he said with awakening eyes.

"That's right," I acknowledged with wonder.

Then Jake was quiet again. He didn't stir all night. And I was glad for his healing.

The next morning, I sat with coffee in hand and looked out at the sky. Jake sat next to me wrapped in the shawl, like a magical, cosmic cocoon.

"How are you doing this morning?" I asked.

"Fine," he simply replied.

"Are you assimilating all of this?" I checked as he smiled in response, then widely opened the shawl and dotingly wrapped me in with him as a wave of compassion swept over us from the love woven into the yarn.

It had been several days, since Jake received the shawl.

He remained quietly next to me as I worked on my laptop at home, covered from head to toe and perfectly still within it.

Twenty minutes later, I noticed a subtle movement from the corner of my eye.

Then in a game of peek-a-boo, Jake began coming to life.

"I see you," I said of his silliness.

"Eek!" he dove back in.

"I love you," I playfully said to him.

"I know!" he boyishly yelled.

His 'child within' must be healing.

This could take a while.

* * *

In another visit with Marina, the chief appeared in a portal sending energy into the land.

"He is a caretaker of the planet and so are you," Marina interpreted. "You have been chosen to help bring the planet back into balance again by exemplifying the kind of life all humans were meant to have."

"You will restructure her energy grid to a much higher frequency. This will release the karmic debris that is smothering her today. With lots of support from all of us, the earth will be whole again."

Initially, I was intimidated by the magnitude of this vision, but the higher realms were clearly in charge and I was just one of many.

"Also, you must write your book," she continued. "You must focus on healing the planet through sharing your own unique truth. Once finished, you will create the artwork, you will later be shown."

"I really don't have a clue how to write anything interesting," I said.

"You will be given the skills you need as they are meant to unfold," she replied. "Don't worry, we're never alone."

That day, Marina helped me assimilate a new energetic template to fit the higher consciousness I was channeling in and helped me download my Akashic Records to guide me in fulfilling my optimal purpose in life.

As the download began, I found myself in the 'library' where the Akashic Records are kept.

It looked like a scene out of "Harry Potter" as I gazed around in amazement and stood at a very tall counter that came all the way up to my chin.

"This place looks like a medieval library filled with ancient books," I said of the magical storehouse.

"That's how it looks to me too," Marina said in response.

As the Keeper of the Akashic Records, an ancient-looking man, appeared behind the counter, he acknowledged my arrival with a glance and a nod of his head.

A rather large and well-worn volume silently shimmered in as he plucked it, spritely, from the air and dropped it on the counter with an unceremonious thud.

The book was bound in ethereal cloth and the edges were curling in. It reminded me of how I'd imagine a rare and ancient text.

As I reached toward the book, it opened by itself.

I could see the writing in it, a precise style executed by hand. And although, I recognized the script, my ability to comprehend it was blocked within its encoding. Yet, I knew I was somehow receiving everything it said.

"That's so weird," I said to Marina. "I can read it on some level, but my brain isn't processing any of it."

"That's probably a good thing as much of its contents are far beyond what the human mind can grasp," she said.

"Why don't you ask them to incorporate your contracts for this present life into your energy field?"

So I made the request and the energies channelled in.

"Is this entire book for me?" I wondered after that.

"I don't know, why don't you look?" Marina suggested. "It could be just a few pages or more."

So I began flipping through it, by simply 'intending' to see, and sure enough, the entire book was written just for me.

"How could I have so many contracts? There must be thousands of them," I said.

"They go into very fine detail and you've been here a very long time," Marina explained. "So it isn't surprising at all."

"The Akashic Records are humanity's roadmaps," my Higher Self chimed in. "They were written to help humanity stay on course to enlightenment. They also provide conscious awareness of being One with Source."

Then my Akashic Records and the information they held came in through my sixth chakra and several hours later, I could feel their voluminous energies to the very tips of my toes.

* * *

I had grown accustomed to Jake's energies being around all the time. I loved him for the lives we shared and the support we exchanged, energetically.

At times I even wondered, if I was in love with him.

So on a very special night, I tuned into Jake.

"Happy Valentine's Day," I said as he smiled at me in response.

"Are you in love with me?" I asked as he looked a bit confused.

"You know, the way I'm in love with you," I pressed.

He turned directly toward me and spoke very patiently.

"Of course, I love you," he said. "I always have and I always will, but you seem to forget, I am the Higher Self of Jake and comprised of the perfect ethereal template for any ideal man. That's why you're in love with me."

"But my present day personality has been through a lot in this life and has a lot of healing to do. Although, Jake thinks of you kindly, his physical manifestation still carries a lot of fear. In fact, he doesn't feel he should date for at least another three years."

Now, I was a bit confused.

"It's something he read in a book on divorce," he said with a comical shrug.

"I wish, he remembered our lives together, so he could see what I can," I confessed.

Jake's Higher Self outstretched his arms and hugged me with comforting words.

"Patience, my dear, it's all going to be far better than you can imagine."

He woke me later that night with a bright bouquet of ethereal flowers and dotingly kissed the top of my head.

"Jake treats the prayer shawl with reverence. It somehow feels sacred to him," Jake's Higher Self explained. "He senses the unconditional love with which it was created."

"Thank you," I responded and was comforted by his words.

* * *

Not long after, I met with Marina. The imagery was the most beautiful, I had witnessed thus far.

My Higher Self stood in front of me with delicate hands folded reverently in the posture of prayer.

As she placed her luminous hands into my physical heart, she gracefully bowed her head.

And there, she remained in honor of me and my powerful purpose on Earth.

The 'Light' was magnificent.

"This energetic symbolism is proof that your prayers are being answered and that they align with your heart," Marina interpreted.

"You are fully supported by the higher realms."

Now on a much deeper level, I fully understood that staying true to oneself in life is the most important thing.

Regardless of how weird or unique you may see yourself, relationships need to fit your path, not the other way around.

And when you're truly aligned with your heart, the universe always supports you.

Marina noted, the back of my fifth chakra was corded to sparkling energy coming directly from Source. This was clearing any doubt about speaking my own unique truth.

And my first chakra was corded to a magical life force energy creating my optimal path.

"You've been going through something called 'the dark night of the soul,'" Marina interpreted. "But your attitude is so great and your energy so positive that you're sailing right through it. Great job!"

The next day, I thought of my first time on Earth, when humans seeded the planet, and wondered about my name.

So I turned deep inside myself to the infinite stillness within and tuned into the aboriginal facet of my Higher Self.

"What was my name in the lifetime, when the chief was my dad?" I asked, as my beautiful, past life essence appeared in front of me.

She was holding a single, white flower opened to the sun.

Beyond that, I didn't see more.

* * *

At this point, I was seeing Marina almost every week. Our time together was magical and today was no exception.

"I thought it might be fun to see, if we could hear what my name was, when the chief was my dad," I began. "As long as it was my original name in this cycle on Earth, maybe it has some significance."

Marina looked surprised.

"Well, I don't know about asking for something in such detail," she began. "I usually get information in pictures. I've never asked for specifics."

"That's okay," I responded, charmed by her modesty. "If that's not something you think you can do, it's not that big of a deal."

"I don't know," continued Marina, uncharacteristically. "That's very specific and I usually see information in much more general terms.

"Let's just try," I encouraged her. "It might be fun!"

So, Marina gave in, as the chief appeared in the room with us. Glancing at him for extra support, she tuned into the past lifetime when I was his little girl, then asked about my name.

Slightly tilting her head as if trying to better hear, Marina sounded out, "L-L-Lo-t-u-s..."

Then she sat back and took a deep breath.

Now leaning forward, she sounded out, "B-l-o-s-s-o-m..." and noted, it was white.

"White Lotus Blossom... That's it!" she announced.

"Hooray! You did it!" I cheered.

Marina looked a bit relieved and equally satisfied.

"Your name was White Lotus Blossom," she repeated, just to hear it again.

"The chief says, he remembers everything about you, when you were his child."

Then I wondered, if it sounded cliché.

"Not at all, it's a powerful name," Marina answered my thoughts.

Then I confessed, when she first said, "Lotus," I thought of the luxury car.

"Well, intuitive perceptions are typically 90% accurate," she said with a twinkling smile.

I told her, I had tried to figure it out the night before and was shown a single, white flower opened to the sun.

"There you go," said Marina. "You're getting good at this too!"

I asked about Jake. He'd been standing a distance away and now moved closer in. As he fully came into view, he looked like a whirlwind of chaos.

"Jake's going through a lot right now," Marina interpreted.

"I hope, I'm being supportive of him," I said with quiet concern.

"You are," Marina replied.

But then, with deep compassion, she spoke of a trend she had seen.

"Couples with many shared lifetimes are often together to clear themselves as a part of awakening," she explained.

"When you're ready for the kind of relationship you want, a truly magnificent one, there's usually not a lot of history together."

"It seems you and Jake have been together to help one another heal."

I looked at her completely confused and unable to fathom her words.

Marina tuned into both of us, then gave an audible sigh.

"Your Higher Selves just explained that although you have a contract to be together again, you've accomplished all you wanted to do through your unconditional love, so your contract is now complete," she confirmed.

I paused as the news sank in.

"I know, you love Jake very much," Marina continued. "Your love is deeply rooted and spans countless lifetimes on Earth. Often, you have been one another's greatest support, while here."

"And yet, you've been healing so rapidly that you have fulfilled your contract, energetically, so it's time for you to move on to a higher purpose now."

I stared at Marina in disbelief.

"But that's not fair," I responded. "I thought we were healing, so we'd be together. Isn't that what you said?"

Then pausing to swallow the lump in my throat, I continued my heartfelt plea.

"This makes no sense," I protested. "What's the point in all of this, if I'm not going to be with him?"

"I know, it's hard to understand," Marina said, comfortingly. "But this is a spiritual world. You've been together spiritually for quite some time now."

"Keep in mind, the version of Jake you've been with comes from his Higher Self and is not his personality in this present life. He has a lot of healing to do and may not be the best partner for you."

I felt exceedingly miserable as Marina continued to speak.

"You are at a very high level in your purpose here," she explained. "And you need to know, the higher realms don't care about romance right now."

"They're focused on healing the planet through our reawakening. Plus, there's no such thing as male or female in the higher realms; there is only neutrality."

"Jake is helping you clear the way for the one who will suit you best. You won't be alone, I promise," she finished.

"Can you at least double check?" I asked.

"Of course," Marina said.

"Is there anyway, you will be together in this present life?" she asked.

"I'm sorry," Marina said softly. "Your contract is complete. This is a very common way, two closely connected souls assist one another, while on the physical plane."

"Jake has been helping you heal the karma you needed to heal from the past, which has set the stage for your optimal partner to come into your life. It's time for you to move on."

My eyes filled with tears.

Before the session was over, Marina helped me end this chapter in my present life, by removing my old ethereal form and releasing it's residue.

Jake came closer to thank me, and I thanked him as well.

I told him, how precious our time together had been for me again.

Then Marina helped me download a new energetic grid, encoded to bring in the optimal people, places and situations that would best support my path.

In the distance, a new man came to the edge of my energy field, but he kept a respectful distance. Although I noticed him briefly, I didn't welcome the change.

"I am so not ready for some other guy," I said through my welling tears.

"I know you love Jake very much," Marina gently assured. "But you'll have plenty of time to adjust. He's simply here to show his support during this painful transition."

On the drive home, I wept.

I thought Jake and I were healing, so we'd be together again.

Had I known it would end like this…

A decade ago, I had seen my future regarding my island home. I was surrounded by grandchildren, but Jake was nowhere to be found.

At the time, I couldn't believe it, so I rationalized something else; maybe he's out running errands or just in another room. But finally, I accepted the fact that he hadn't been there at all.

At home, I opened my laptop and searched, 'white lotus blossom' in the hope it might serve as a distraction from my broken heart.

An essay on the lotus sutra came up in the search results.

"The white lotus blossom symbolizes the pacification of one's earthly nature in the physical realm. It is the state of bodhi that serves as the womb from which the world rebirths into purification."

"Out of the swamp (physicality) and murky waters (emotion), it rises into the air (thoughts) and aspires toward the light of the sun (creation) as it blossoms into a vivid white flower."

"It is symbolic of the means to enlightenment."

"Well, at least it has a nice meaning," I consoled myself.

* * *

When I started meditating, and for many years after that, I was drawn to the sages of ancient wisdom and other clear-sighted souls. I wanted to emulate present day healers, along with my favorite fictional characters; Neo and Yoda, of course.

But as I compared myself to others, as a way of measuring-up, I realized something in contrast to this.

We are each meant to add our own piece to the puzzle in every single life by embodying our own unique gifts and not emulating others.

Letting go of goal-images, based on anyone else, helped me fully self-actualize into the best version of myself.

Chapter Six

The Moon

I was feeling exceptionally glum. I had weathered the loss of my marriage and lost all of my wealth. I had sent my kids off to college and in a very unusual way, I had fallen in love.

I awoke the next morning and noticed the vacant room.

Jake was nowhere to be found.

For more than a year, he'd been with me in spirit, greeting me every morning, laughing along with me. He had stayed with my energy field to help me heal synergistically.

Now I was alone.

I wept at the emptiness around me and loneliness I felt.

"Jake, are you there?" I softly called out.

In the silence, no answer came.

"Will you be okay?" I asked.

From afar, his familiar voice sounded in great distress.

"I'm fine," was all he could muster, then not another word.

So I continued to bolster myself with positive thoughts and words.

"I have to have faith," I encouraged myself. "I have to stay focused and trust. This, of all times, is when my faith in myself should be the strongest."

That night, I quietly wept and with each tear came relief.

Soon, there was only silence as I lay fast asleep, when Jake appeared in the still of the night and kissed me on the cheek.

I continued to feel very much alone and had little desire to go out and distract myself with friends. How could I speak of my broken heart? Would my story go something like this?

"You see, there's this guy from college and I recently saw him again. We danced at a friend's wedding, but I never heard from him."

"Unexpectedly, he stayed with me, energetically. Well, technically, it wasn't him. It was the multi-dimensional matrix that comprises his consciousness comes."

"Anyway, he's super sweet and we've been in love many times. In fact, we had an agreement to get together again, but we've done everything we were meant to do, just with our energy fields (that's how amazing we are together). So in the end, we said goodbye, and my heart is completely broken."

This was how I was feeling and I wanted to tell everyone. But I knew as much as I was adored, my story would sound insane. So I spent my evenings at home alone and focused on work instead.

As the days passed, it wasn't long before my heavy heart lightened and signs of healing began. Tears welled in my eyes when I realized, my heart would indeed, soon mend, and I would no longer miss him.

It's just that I didn't want this time of loving him to end.

Ironically, I would see the 'real' Jake for the first time in over a year. Friends were hosting a graduation and Jake was flying in.

While on a walk that afternoon, I thought about the chief. I wanted to carry the medicine that guides one over the sacred bridge that shifts one's place of 'being' from the head into the heart. So I asked, if I could carry it and pass it on to Jake.

That evening, a surge of energy came pouring into my head, so intensely that I had to lie down, until I could function again.

The frequency was so voluminous, it felt like my head would explode, but I knew the chief was supporting me and gave into the massive download.

I awoke the next morning with infinite love from within.

I wasn't the slightest bit nervous, when I arrived to see my friends.

I hadn't seen Jake since the wedding, and my heart raced excitedly, yet my heightened presence was perfectly calm as I kept my focus on the objective of passing the medicine on.

"He's the most gorgeous man I've ever seen," I thought as I tripped on the grass, traversing the yard to greet him. But he ignored my not-so-graceful move as his twinkling eyes welcomed me.

As we greeted one another and our conversation began, an age-old-rhythm arose as it had countless times before.

"Cup-a-Joe?" he asked, when dessert came around.

"Sure," I said, smiling at him.

"How do you like it?" he asked.

"A little cream," I said.

"I'm coming back in October for our class reunion," he added as he walked off to oblige.

Nothing of significance happened that night, just a simple reminder I'd see him again. But I knew our time had passed, despite my love for him, and with every glance between us, the medicine traveled to him.

When the evening came to an end, I gave Jake an extra-long hug goodbye. And as I stepped into the cool night air, I wished him happiness.

The chief appeared and walked by my side as I thanked him for his assistance. Then once in my car, I quietly wept and completely let go of Jake.

Later that night, I awoke to find Jake's Higher Self by my bed. He looked as he did in our first lifetime, when the chief was my dad.

He had the same eyes and refined, rugged presence. His thick, dark hair was pulled back in a braid, adorned with a single, blue feather.

As he looked into my questioning eyes, he lovingly smiled at me.

"I'm in my medicine time now," he wanted me to know.

He would transform in solitude.

This was a sacred path.

When I awoke the next morning, Jake was further out. His appearance was visibly stronger as his soul began to awaken.

His ethereal journey would be greatly transformative and I trusted the chief would watch over him like a father would his son.

For another night, Jake stood in the distance and lovingly watched over me.

"I'm alright now," I assured him. "Thanks for giving me time to adjust. As always, I love you forever."

As I finished my final goodbye, his image began to fade. It rose into the evening sky as a twinkle among the infinite stars illuminating the heavens.

Quietly, I said goodnight on the ethereal plane, and from the place where Jake once stood, my daughter sweetly reached out to me and gently took my hand.

The following day, I sat in the living room drinking my afternoon tea. I was struggling to envision what would come next as the chief appeared in the room.

"Drink your tea, write your book and open yourself to abundance," he said. "The Great Spirit always provides for you and this will never change."

I thought of how simple life had been, when we first seeded the planet during utopian times.

"I wish you were still my dad," I thoughtfully reminisced.

And from a distance, not distant at all, the chief spoke patiently.

"I have always been your dad and I will always be. But you don't need me in your life, you simply need yourself," he explained.

"You need yourself to take care of you and be strong, loving and kind. You need to give yourself a feeling of safety and confidence, and you need to fully self-actualize and you can have Shalom (peace)."

That night, I watched "The Matrix." Who could resist Keanu Reeves? It was the first grownup movie I let my children see (while fast-forwarding through the icky parts).

"This is the way the world really is," I told my exceptional kids. "It's a metaphor for the brain's programming (the perception of a physical world) within which, the human ego (the relentless Agent Smiths) keep us trapped in mental loops by creating continuous fear.

Beyond this, is the world of enlightenment (freedom of consciousness) through which Neo regains his clarity and optimal power on Earth."

The next night, I felt little motivation, so I watched "50 First Dates." I cried at the end when they got together, despite Lucy's short-term memory loss.

Like most of the world, Jake suffered from memory loss as well. Although his short-term memory (of his present life) remained fully intact, his memories of our many past lives were the ones I wished he had.

Most of us don't remember the people we've loved in past lives, it's true. But most of our past life emotions remain on a cellular level. 'Love at first sight' happens to us, when we meet someone we already love in another dimension or time.

"You have become a master of accepting what is," Marina said the following day. "And you're connected to 'still-point energy.' This is the place from which all miracles manifest on the physical plane."

"You've also achieved a sense of 'total security within the insecurity' of your life's circumstances and in the world."

I thought of the scene in "The Matrix" in which Neo appears to be dead, but with Trinity's faithful insistence, he magically comes back to life as a 'Master of the

Matrix' and disarms the bullets fired at him with calm and quizzical ease.

"This new perspective is a very important theme for your path," Marina explained. "It shows a depth of stillness rarely achieved in life."

This was the place of peace at which, I had now arrived. I was completely confident in my own unique path in life and had no fear regarding my unusual clarity. In fact, I was happy for it and knew wondrous things lie ahead.

In the next few days, I experienced another energy shift. It was the final assimilation of my Walk-In into my physical form.

So I thanked my Higher Self for all the miracles in my life. Then abruptly, I was very aware of also being my Higher Self and hearing myself saying "thank you" to me from my present life.

Had I experienced multiple points of consciousness all at once?

As time went on, I realized, I had needed a broken heart. There had been a hard shell around it for many centuries. Even though I loved my best, my love in this realm wasn't pure; it was mixed with fear, ego, pride, anger and uncertainty.

So my broken heart was a great release and massively healing for me. Once shattered, I gathered the pieces of it in my ethereal hands and examined their energies.

In this fragmented state, my broken heart's limitations were easily neutralized.

And I watched with fascination as a much better heart reassembled itself automatically.

A few months later, I was steady at the helm. Jake passed in and out of my thoughts, but life was busy and things were good.

"The planet's going through a major shift right now," Marina explained over tea. "Rather than trying to 'fix' one another, we're each meant to fix ourselves. We no longer need to take responsibility for others, but allow them to make their own choices in life."

"We should accept one another as each in their own divine process. Who are we to come between someone and their own creations?"

The chief appeared with another peace pipe in his powerful hands. It symbolized using one's unique voice to align with their optimal purpose.

And through a guided meditation, I learned more about my path.

As my aboriginal facet on the spiritual plane, I stood in my sacred place on Sanibel Island again. The sun shone on my radiant skin and the breeze flowed through my hair. The waves washed over my delicate feet as I firmly stood in the sand.

The chief appeared on my left and my kids boldly stood on my right. I was shown, my work right now was a momentary phase. My primary divine purpose had to do with healing the Earth.

My guides appeared with a chalice, then placed it in my heart. It contained the essential energies in support of my optimal path.

Aboriginals are the earthbound spirits that humans are meant to be. They walk the earth in balance and live in harmony with all existence here. They listen to their own inner voice and look within for all guidance, while creating their destiny.

"I see the Creator in you," they knowingly greet one another.

That evening, I settled into a comfy chair to meditate. Jake appeared in the room. I hadn't seen him in months.

He bowed and placed his hands on my cheeks, then aligned his 6th chakra (third eye) directly with my own as his pure and unconditional love flooded my consciousness.

Instinctively, I closed my eyes, allowing myself to be open to receiving his loving support. So powerful was his faith in me that tears gently rolled down my cheeks.

"You can do this," he said with confidence.

"I know," I replied with ease.

I was in a beautiful place and learning a new way to view myself as an instrument on Earth.

"If you tighten the strings too much, they will snap. If you leave them too slack, they won't play," I heard Siddhartha's sweet presence fine-tuning my system that day. "Remember the middle path, dear one. Neutrality is the way."

I had loved every moment of raising my kids. They were my greatest joy. More important than anything else I could teach them was how to guide themselves.

When they were puzzled and asked for advice, I often responded with something redundant or something they already knew. Routinely, they looked disappointed and said my advice was lame.

"Listen to your own voice," I would say, encouraging them to think for themselves. "You have all the answers you need."

"But how?" they would ask, completely annoyed.

"Imagine a perfect version of 'you' sitting next to yourself," I'd explain. "Now ask your 'perfect presence' the question you just asked me, and listen to what you say.

A perfect version of your true self is really who you are and the optimal answer to any question always comes from your heart."

This 'imaginary' exercise circumnavigates the brain's control software and keeps your ego at bay. It helps you hear your own unique voice, free from societal programming.

Plus, merging with your perfect presence (that which you truly are), helps you raise your frequency to optimal clarity.

That night, I met the moon. Could my life get any weirder?

While walking my dogs at dusk, I caught a glimpse of the moon. It was round and full as it rose in the sky with a captivating iridescence.

As I stood there gazing, its radiant energies gently filled my earthly consciousness.

And then without warning it happened.

It was totally out of the blue.

I watched as a wisp of golden light swooped playfully down from the moon.

It danced along the boulevard until it revealed itself.

And I knew this familiar presence, as if I always had.

She appeared in the grass before me, as a luminous child.

I stared at her in disbelief.

She was 'Spirit Moon.'

"I just had to come down and meet you," she said in a clear, little voice.

I was charmed by her whimsical air, but far too stunned to reply. She was a striking departure from Mother Earth's presentation and style.

As the sweet little spirit bowed, I instinctively did the same as our divine consciousness merged into being One.

"Mutual love and honor comprise the higher realms," she transmitted.

And with this brief encounter, she twinkled a gentle goodbye, then vanished up into the night.

"What a beautiful little light," I thought and continued to walk my dogs.

The following evening, on my drive home, the moon rose into the sky. Charmed by meeting her previously, I looked at the moon and smiled.

Instantly, Spirit Moon was sitting next to me in the car.

She took my hand as her cosmic energies coursed throughout my form.

"How are you?" I asked, once I was able to speak.

"I'm good!" the spirit replied.

Her energy was so up-lifting, I felt completely refreshed.

"Where do you come from?" I asked.

"The same place as you," she replied. "Unified Consciousness. You know, we're the same, you and I. And did you know the source of existence is unconditional love?"

"Although it sounds redundant, I'm beginning to figure that out," I said, enchanted by her wisdom.

I asked if she needed to heal, like Mother Earth's request.

"No, I don't," she answered. "I am pristine creation and remain as I've always been; pure, divine consciousness."

I had a wonderful time with Marina the following day.

My first chakra was corded to a vast amount of my own divine essence, filling me with nourishing light. And from my ethereal presence, Marina was shown the next step toward healing humanity.

We could see that fear and manipulation are epidemic today, but this next step in healing ourselves would free us from victimization.

For thousands of years, governments, corporations and other profiteers have used and abused the public as captive revenue streams.

Now, my guides were showing Marina a special protocol that disengages humanity from societal predators.

As the clearing began, J.P. Morgan popped in. He started the Federal Reserve that secretly funds the wars and corruption hidden from public view.

"Why do we have a federal government?" I asked. "Why aren't we just 'the united states' like the unified countries of Europe with revenue for self-governance only taxed within each state?"

"Then we'd avoid the stockpile of money in Washington D.C. that attracts endless corruption and unsavory profiteers."

"Some of our founding fathers had a lot more integrity than politicians today," Marina explained. "Now, Capitol Hill is wrought with corruption and uses tax payers' money to fund lots of greedy self-interest and other despicable deeds."

I was becoming more aware of my infinite consciousness.

I realized, we as divine presence are barely in this realm.

We are also doing other things in many unique dimensions.

The physical world is far too basic to keep our infinite consciousness engaged for very long.

It's 'basic' because most humans are stuck in a low vibrational fog.

This is caused by lack of self-forgiveness (letting go of the past), lack of self-love (loving oneself unconditionally) and the brain's insatiable desire to control our lives on Earth.

But the brain only knows, what the brain only knows.

It can't create anything new.

Creation comes from our Higher Selves that animate us on Earth.

Allowing the brain to be in charge keeps us stuck in vibrational loops that block our inherent clarity and infinite consciousness.

'Unified presence' is the goal of our current awakening.

At this frequency, nothing exists, but resonant harmony.

Communication is telepathic and therefore, absolute.

Peace and perfection are inherent in all creation on Earth.

Could this be achievable as a species again in the world?

How much of the world's complexity does the average human perceive? How conscious are we of the systems inherent in life on this beautiful planet?

For example, thanks to Isaac Newton, we know that all objects in existence attract one another. This magnetic force is based on the mass of each individual object and the distance between the two. The larger the mass and shorter the distance, the stronger the force will be.

So the massive body of the Earth creates gravitational pull, while all existence upon its surface attracts to the planet as well. Due to this attraction (ie. gravity) we happily live our lives on Earth, while spinning upon her surface at speeds approaching 1,000 mph (at the equator).

The moon is also drawn to the earth and gravity holds it near as it endlessly orbits the planet at 2,288 mph.

And along with this, the earth is also grounding itself to the sun, while together we fly through outer space at 67,000 mph. Yet, we hardly notice this.

Are the vast mechanical systems that comprise the universe beyond the capability of human consciousness?

Are we, by nature, predisposed to live in oblivion?

Is that why we're so easily duped by predatory illusion?

Another night, while driving home, the moon appeared again. As before, I was charmed.

"You're right about attraction, it's inherent in everything," Spirit Moon began. "And we can alter the course of it with our focused intention."

"Regarding travel, there are no fossil fuels in the higher realms. We simply create magnetic pull by putting forth an intention that encodes our energy fields to where we want to go."

"Via this encoding, we tune into what we want and chart our optimal course. We traverse from one place to the next via portals of intention."

"What about time and space, do they exist anywhere else?" I asked.

"Soon you will see, these physical concepts don't exist at all," she replied. "They are simply a human illusion."

I had a wonderful time with Marina several days after that. My aura was filled with pink (healed heart) and violet (Higher Self).

My second chakra was corded to a bright, positive energy that was helping me achieve my purpose in this particular life.

My fifth chakra (speaking my truth) was corded to my right occiput (the right and left occiputs are the portals through which we enter and exit the physical body as spirit).

A vast amount of my own divine essence was streaming into me with a cord at my left occiput with new perceptions of reality gently flowing in.

My heart (fourth chakra) was corded to my Walk-In (my 'Unity Self') that was merging with my physical form and weaving complex unity frequencies into my energy grid.

And my Unity Self would soon be my guide as my present day self from within.

In an elaborate vision the next afternoon, I traveled to the Utopia of Unification from which my Walk-In originates.

After traveling a great distance through my consciousness, I discovered Marina, the chief and my kids standing there to greet me.

They smiled as I looked around in surprise and began tuning into the place.

As I allowed my energy field to match the unity vibe, I noticed, I was standing exactly where I had been all along. The only distance I'd traveled was through the programming in my mind.

And I realized that in consciousness, not only are we One, but all dimensions, places and times are in every cell of existence.

By healing the various levels of our own subconscious mind, we can easily tune our energy fields (just like a radio dial) to align with whatever we want to experience in the physical realm, as the tiniest speck of our energy holds infinity and beyond.

Soon October arrived, along with my college reunion.

For months, I had looked forward to it, mainly because of Jake, but now my attention had shifted to my study abroad classmates.

When I walked into the banquet hall, Jake was already seated with a new friend. From across the room, he flagged me down. As I approached, he smiled, then gave me a giant hug and asked if I had also come with anyone of interest.

"I'm here with my Nottingham group," I referred to my junior year abroad.

"I wish, I would have traveled, when I was young," he said.

"You still can," I responded to this.

"But it isn't the same at this age," he replied.

"I know," I agreed with him. "You don't have to live on a shoe string and you can travel in style. You can even stay in nice hotels and eat in fancy restaurants."

We both laughed at this obvious truth.

He thanked me for the prayer shawl, I'd knit for him in the spring.

"I'm sorry, I didn't say anything earlier," Jake shyly explained. "I didn't know what to say at first, it's absolutely beautiful."

"I still can't get over the detail of the fly-fishing hooks with the fish on them. It must have been a lot of work and I couldn't believe anyone would do such a nice thing for me."

"Well, I knew you were going through a rough time and thought you should know people care," I responded with eyes twinkling.

Shortly after our conversation, I joined my Nottingham friends.

My time with Jake was only a moment and I would most likely not see him again.

Several days later, I was drinking a cup of tea. A portal opened in which I saw myself sitting on a beach, reading my book to humanity.

My second chakra instructed me to go to my occiput, where my guides (the various facets of my expanding consciousness) were sending the narrative, I was destined to write. Their support was now apparent to me; they were the authors of my story and I was simply a scribe.

"Your book will end with a single graphic with triggers encoded within to activate realignment with humanity's sacred heart. This will help those who read your book live conscious lives again," the higher realms explained.

And with this, they released my doubts regarding my optimal path and I was shown my true story was already well received.

"You are a living example of the future of humankind," the higher realms continued. "Because you are no longer veiled in your physical mind, your existence in all dimensions will soon be apparent to you."

"Your multidimensional consciousness and the expansive perspective it brings will assimilate into your everyday life and become your normal view."

"Am I free to share my story without calling it science fiction?" I asked.

"You are," the higher realms confirmed. "All of your experience, now exists in collective mind. Your truth will be self-evident and they will hear you this time."

"This time?" I questioned the heavens as my guides knowingly smiled.

We are all multidimensional beings and manifestations of Source; the portal of 'Light' comprised of all consciousness merged into One.

When we 'see the light' or 'go into the light' as we pass from our physical lives, we are returning through the same portal from which we came into our lives. We're transitioning out of linear time (in which the concepts of time and space have measurable characteristics) and fully into the present (ie. nonlinear time).

But when our earthly consciousness exits the physical mind (a very slow vibe), its filters slow our transition down, so we can have time to adjust. This is why we experience the portal as a transitional tunnel, instead of a flash of light (what it truly is), so our brain-based perspective has time to adjust from 'reality' on a timeline to the nonlinear realm.

But in truth, portals have no depth nor time through which we traverse. They are simply a shift in frequency within our consciousness and they happen in a flash. Have you ever heard the expression, "my life flashed before my eyes" when someone goes through this portal as they pass from their physical life?

Surprised by all of this information swirling around in my brain, I paused and began to reason; so if time is truly nonlinear and Source is a portal of Light, is the light it projects as the universe (the substance of which everything is comprised) just another portal that only exists in the present?

If so, is our entire earthly existence just a flash of light?

Chapter Seven

The Rock

One morning I awoke, randomly thinking of Jesus Christ.

Despite my expanding awareness, remnant Christian beliefs had remained deep within my psyche.

I never used God's name in vain and adhered to biblical guidelines, due to a lingering subconscious fear that I may not be worthy of heaven.

Then I remembered my first clairvoyant from over a decade before.

"You were once a young man in the closest circle of Jesus' friends during his life on Earth," she said with emphasis.

Powerful feelings began to stir, from a mix of past life memories I hadn't yet seen.

Chills ran up and down my spine.

Had I actually known him?

Still in bed, I sat up and piled pillows behind my back, then closed my eyes and took a deep breath as I turned my attention within.

"Was I alive during Jesus' life?" I asked the ether around me. 'If so, then what was my name?"

"Peter" rang out in the room.

The audible word was crisp and clear, the sound of it startled me.

"Was I one of Jesus' disciples?" I wondered after that.

So I searched 'the twelve disciples' on my phone and a list of them came up: Simon, Andrew, James, John, Philip, Bartholomew, Thomas, Matthew, another James, Thaddeus, another Simon and Judas.

But 'Peter' was not on the list, so I asked with more conviction.

"Who was I during Jesus' life?" I asked the heavens above.

"Peter" echoed the sound again.

So I searched "Jesus and Peter" on my phone and read the narrative.

"You mean the disciple Simon as in Simon Peter?" I asked and heard a sigh of relief as I finally understood.

But this was preposterous.

So, I reviewed this new information with my logical mind…

The church I attended while growing up was "St. Peter's Lutheran Church…"

Could the suggestive subconscious mind be this precise and intense?

And I disregarded the notion.

The next morning, I sat down to meditate and did my usual clearing on myself and my kids as my divine essence arose from deep within my presence.

As it did, I felt Simon's energy filling my consciousness and for a brief moment, I experienced his likeness within my own and was struck by the similarities.

"Could I have been Simon Peter?" I cautiously entertained, quite aware of the notion sounding completely ridiculous.

But I had learned that past lifetimes served as modes of healing and personal paradigms greatly impact our intuitive perceptions.

Could this be my subconscious way of releasing unwanted programming by merging with collective perspectives of a biblical figure?

During our lives, we receive information through many modalities. And when we remember past lifetimes, we perceive them as uniquely our own to fully assimilate any energies beneficial for us.

But if they were truly our past lives or not (the more likely perspective for me), has yet to be determined.

So, if I was Simon or not, didn't matter to me, nor did it seem relevant. Either way, I had lots of new information coming in and I had learned to trust the process.

So I gave into it.

As I adjusted to the presence of Simon Peter that day, the memories of his life were revealed as if they had happened to me.

But soon I became confused by the gross disparities; his life as I now remembered it, greatly contradicted the history books I had read.

So I sat down in a quiet place, took a deep breath and turned within.

"I really don't know what's happening," I confessed to the ether that day, regarding my new awareness of this person in history.

And before I finished the thought, a portal encompassed me as I stood in another time and place that had altered history.

The time was 325 A.D., hundreds of years after Simon had lived, and at first I didn't understand, what I was doing there.

But as the vision progressed, I grew deeply entranced as I witnessed a moment in history of unforeseen magnitude that would alter the course of human awareness for nearly two thousand years.

Instinctively, I knew the scene was 'The Council of Nicaea'.

Emperor Constantine stood at a table surrounded by powerful men. Too furious to sit down, he loudly pounded his fist and shouted at the council before him.

Enraged by the haphazard systems for governing his vast lands, he demanded a form of unification to save his crumbling kingdom and harness his human conquests in perpetuity.

So the council of clever advisors suggested various plans. They would enlarge their militia by recruiting the poor and those on the fringes of every society.

"That isn't enough," the emperor roared. "I want complete control!"

Then with fierce intimidation, he snarled, "I want every minion within my domain skewered, roasted and served on a platter; I want their very souls!"

Now at this time in history, most of the dissension in the Roman Empire was due to the vast array of cultures and ideologies they had conquered over the years.

The masses were mostly free-thinking and held nature-based, pagan and mythological views.

Egyptian and Greek mythologies were accepted by most as real and everyone, except the Greeks, still thought the earth was flat and even believed the sun and the planets revolved around the world.

After long deliberation, the council came up with a plan. They would secure control of their conquests through their core belief systems by mixing and merging existing views into a modern religion.

So they concocted a new world order of blended storylines and in the retelling, they targeted a past and beloved rabbi from hundreds of years before.

They said, he was conceived of a virgin, impregnated by a god, then sacrificed by his heavenly father to save the world from the ravages of suffering after death.

Now, the construct of a savior-figure (a theoretical entity) had been a proven strategy in many societies and served a dual purpose for them.

First, the belief in a savior-figure and divinely conceived demigod would subjugate everyone else as inferior and flawed, and condition them to depend on the guidance of holy superiors.

Secondly, in John 3:16 the Holy Bible reads: "For God so loved the world, that he gave his only begotten son, that whosoever believes in him should not perish, but have everlasting life."

With such a distressing notion planted in the minds of those he ruled, parents would send their sons to war, without knowing the reasons why, and forfeit the lives of their innocent children (as God forfeited Christ), when proclaimed by higher authorities to be for the greater good.

This same technique is often used by governments today, who promote conflict around the world with 'good vs. evil' misinformation, then send their 'heroic defenders' off to fight in foreign lands, when in truth, their missions are secretly suited to robbers, killers and thugs.

So the council created illusions of hierarchy on Earth.

They anointed saints, popes and priests as their corps of religious enforcers.

They would rule the entire world by deeming the masses inherently flawed and condemned to burning in hell, unless they bowed to their army of holy superiors.

They claimed Simon Peter was sanctified with direct permission from God as the head of their Roman Church.

Then shortly thereafter they crucified him (upside-down) and buried him under the Vatican, so one of their newly anointed popes could rule the world instead.

But I was shown via Simon's awareness, all of this was false. He was never in Rome, nor was he ever martyred.

In fact, he died quite peacefully, at the age of 63, near the small town of Fatih (in Istanbul, Turkey today).

I remembered his final moments with perfect clarity. He was surrounded by those he loved and filled with the deep satisfaction of a good life well spent.

So with many illusions planted into the minds of those he ruled, Constantine launched his strategy with the calculated brutality of a militarized zone.

He went after the wealth of the lands and the people with threats of hellfire and damnation, unless they paid his new religion's salvation-based taxation.

And this is how the Roman Church actually began.

The Roman Empire didn't 'fall' as the history books suggest, but surreptitiously shifted its power into a government church and unleashed its unconscionable greed as the will of 'The God of All Gods.'

Religion was Constantine's tour de force that ensnared the human heart, irrespective of culture and borders, he subjugated his conquests in perpetuity.

And today, his ancient empire, under the guise of the Roman Church, remains one of the wealthiest schemes ever concocted on Earth.

* * *

I emailed Marina the following day and told her what I had seen.

"You're on the right track," she answered. "You also might want to take a look at the 'Essenes' and who you were back then."

So I sat down in a quiet place, took a deep breath and turned within as a portal of light appeared.

Deep within the vision, I was Simon again.

I remembered the day Simon met Jesus, with perfect clarity. Simon and his brother, Andrew, were fishing by the sea.

And on that day, when Jesus met Simon, he notably called him the 'Rock' ("Kepha" in Aramaic) meaning - 'a small stone that has broken off from the massive ledge,' acknowledging Simon's pure and inherent freedom-of-consciousness.

Simon had remained unshackled by predatory illusion and other collective vibes.

Much later, according to oral traditions, 'Kepha' morphed into 'Petros' as the stories were told in Greek, which became the name, Peter, we use in English today.

But during his life, he was only known as Shimon ('to hear') Bar Yonah ('spirit').

Then as I stood next to Andrew, I was drawn deeply into his eyes and reminded of a friend in this life, who had triggered my own inner journey with his cathartic insight, "You cause all your own problems."

No wonder I trusted him now.

I awoke the next morning with thoughts of past life regression and how a simple intention can shift one's awareness to the vibration where all the answers lie.

Whether this is experienced on a conscious level or not, it happens to everyone. Through these energetic connections, we learn and evolve in the physical realm, continually attracting, downloading and assimilating energies of all kinds.

The following day, Marina called.

"How are you processing things?" she asked. "I was in that lifetime, too. There's a lot of misinformation about our beliefs back then."

"What do you mean by 'our beliefs'?" I asked.

"We were the Essenes," Marina said. "We knew that every creature is divine presence on Earth, taking shape in a physical form. Unlike most, we were not held captive by predatory illusion."

"There's a group that's been getting together. I think you should meet them too. It's a group of friends who were with us back then. And I think it would help to have their support while you're making these paradigm shifts. I know it's a lot to take in right now, but your memories will become clearer as you process everything," she explained.

It had been a week, since I connected with Simon's consciousness. Along with all the new information, every time I thought of Marina, Mary Magdalene came to mind.

So I called her one afternoon and told her what I was seeing, and wondered how she would react to my bizarre perception.

"You're very intuitive," Marina said. "Memorable people in history, such as Mary Magdalene, were often comprised of a vast collective of many unique souls. You are seeing this same consciousness in my energy field today."

"For real?" I asked, a bit overwhelmed and not really sure what to think.

"Yes," Marina answered. "I was one of many souls who comprised Mary Magdalene. And just like you, I remember that life with surprising clarity."

"I'd really like you to meet some friends, who were Essenes as well," she continued. "We're meeting tomorrow night at my house. I think you would really enjoy them."

The following night, I arrived at her home just before 7pm. With a mix of excitement and trepidation, I knocked on the door of her condo.

"I'm glad you made it," Marina said and graciously welcomed me in.

After taking my coat, she paused for a moment, then spoke in a quiet tone.

"There's something I need to tell you, and it may come as a shock. But in order for you to break free from illusion, there's something you need to know," she explained. "Jesus didn't die on the cross."

"What?" I looked at Marina.

All time had suddenly stopped, when a cute little lady smiled at me and approached from the living room.

"Uncle Simon!" she said with the joy of a child and the brightest, sparkling eyes.

"Sarah?" I blurted on reflex as I looked into her eyes.

Sarah was Jesus and Mary's daughter, a child the last time we met.

"I'd like you to meet Martha," Marina introduced us. "As you recall, she was my daughter, when we were the Essenes."

"It's so nice to see you again," I said and gave her a giant hug.

Martha wistfully took my arm and led me to the living room to introduce the others.

As I greeted each of them, I instantly recognized Jesus' brother James, James' wife and their son, respectively.

As the evening progressed, I felt noticeably numb as predatory illusion neutralized in my brain.

Then it all came back to me as the jolt of hearing the truth again freed me from illusion and with rapid-fire succession, I remembered everything.

Jesus was actually tied to a single, upright pike (not a cross). There were no nails in his hands nor was there a sword to his side. We gave him herbs, while he was there, to ease some of the pain and gradually sedated him until he was fast asleep.

After the crowd dispersed that night, we gently took him down and carried him home to rest. We left that place when he was able and never returned again.

As the truth reawakened within my consciousness, I realized, that's why the bible skips the burial rituals we would have done. That's why his tomb was found empty. Jesus was really alive.

"I know there's a group assembling that's shutting this paradigm down. It's held people in a victim mentality for nearly 2,000 years," Marina announced that night.

"It's crazy how one bad apple, like Constantine, can alter the truth on such a massive scale."

"Maybe the word 'conman' was coined after Constantine," I said as the women laughed.

But despite my realizations, I remained in total shock.

When I returned home that night, I knew I'd remembered the truth, but the thought of Jesus not being my savior was inconceivable.

Then again, I thought of the telephone game, I had played as a child, and realized many truths can be altered over thousands of years.

* * *

The following week, I met with Marina. As soon as we sat down, Simon's ethereal form appeared and wanted our fullest attention.

"Jesus tried to help everyone awaken their consciousness, but they couldn't assimilate what he said, due to societal programming blocking their clarity," he began.

"Few people could hear there is nothing to fear beyond the physical realm and that all are created equally in the image of the gods."

"Humans were given intelligence to care for the rest of the world. We were not meant to dominate nor do any creature harm. Humans are not superior to any existence here, no more than the earth is the center of the infinite universe."

"So later, we changed our message to something, we hoped might do some good, and enhanced our watered-down message with examples of our divinity, through focused intention and energy work, based on our knowledge of alchemy."

"We emphasized that eternal life is inherent in who we are, but the people were heavily programmed and just couldn't grasp the truth," he said.

Then Simon looked directly at me and spoke in a serious tone.

"It's time for the truth to assimilate. We are counting on you for this," he said. "The planet is in crisis. Humanity must realign with the truth before it destroys itself."

After a moment of silence, he spoke to both of us.

"Jesus' original message was one of self-forgiveness to release our subconscious debris. We are each portals of consciousness and remain divine while here."

"In fact, we are each the sole creator of our own destiny, but the lower vibrations are blocking people's inherent abilities."

"Jesus was here to help us remember who we really are, and that love is unconditional, no matter what happens in life. We are forgiven without exception and always return to the gods from whom we originate."

Simon looked at me again, then spoke with laser-precision.

"It was through the fabrications of the Council of Nicaea that the presiding powers entrenched themselves in the psyche of the masses," he explained.

"With predatory illusions, they wove elaborate energy matrices into collective grids and programmed humanity into being their subservient mechanism."

"This is why Constantine's strategy has thrived among the masses for nearly two thousand years, while other ancient mythologies have faded over time, by keeping them trapped in a fear paradigm with illusions of suffering."

"The 'Sacred Knowledge' inherent in us has been blocked from the physical mind, but we must realign with the truth again," he boldly emphasized.

* * *

Not long after, I met with Marina for lunch. We talked about our memories of our lives as the Essenes.

"I know it will take some time for people to accept that Jesus was simply punished and exiled," Marina said, sensing my lingering shock. "It was common knowledge back then. But there's nothing from which we need to be saved in the afterlife. The only form of 'hell' that exists is suffering in the world."

"There are many things about our existence that can't be put into words. Such concepts are far beyond the structure of language and the mind. But people must realize the truth, each in their own unique way, and the truth shall set them free."

"Despite church claims, Jesus' bloodline didn't end with his life," Marina explained. "Our family traveled to India, then later on to France, where our daughter had children of her own and lived a quiet and peaceful life near Saintes-Maries-de-la-Mer."

Then a portal opened to show the lives of every unique soul, as the higher realms made it perfectly clear, our consciousness matters most.

"We are all the divine lineage of Creative Consciousness here," the higher realms explained. "Hierarchy and inequality are fabrications for greed and gain. But the matrix of programmed illusion is coming to an end. People are reawakening to inherent truths within and soon we will evolve past illusion and never be duped again."

* * *

The world is pure and unfiltered in the eyes of an innocent child. I always trusted my kids' point of view and the beauty of evolution. As I look back on my life, my kids were my greatest teachers.

One day, I was visiting with my son, who was home on a college break. I was sharing my thoughts about writing a book and trusted his gifted perspective. I wondered, what value my story could possibly bring to the world today.

"Will everyone think I'm crazy? Or could my story help bring humanity back into balance again?" I asked. "Could it help us regain our care and compassion for the world?"

"I think your ideas have merit, Mom," my son replied, knowingly. "But why would people want to change, so the world is in balance again?"

I shrugged in response to this.

"To be happy!" he told me, wistfully.

"You're right," I agreed with him.

* * *

A few days later, over a cup of tea, Marina reminded me that I was being forced along my path, but I'd never been much for change.

"The higher realms are squeezing you out financially," she perceived. "They will do so, until you make the choices aligned with your destiny."

"I wish they would lighten up a bit, their techniques are rather harsh," I complained.

"The world is in crisis," Marina reasoned. "There's no time to spare right now."

As I processed Simon's energies over the following weeks, a conflict arose between the truth as I remembered it and my cellular programming.

The belief that a human sacrifice (Christ) was needed to save everyone was so deeply rooted in my subconscious, my body went into shock.

Not only was I processing these conflicting energies, but a flood of collective beliefs and illusions were streaming into me.

Massive amounts of suffering were bombarding my energy field and overwhelming my physical presence. I was clearing collective grids and implants from the past two thousand years via my first chakra and the process became overwhelming.

To top it off, my mother died very suddenly and the resulting familial download added to my distress.

I was also filled with fear regarding what my perspective might bring, so I drove up north to stay by the lake and spend some time with my dad.

Despite the peaceful surroundings, I remained extremely ill, due to collective energies building up in my first chakra.

My intestinal tract completely shut down with the karmic weight it now held as my condition soon grew unbearable and I lived in continuous pain. Miserable days turned into weeks, then months of suffering.

Finally, I asked the heavens to put me out of my misery, but instead of a giant lightning bolt happily striking me dead, my mother appeared before me as a perfect ethereal presence.

"You must have faith," she comforted me. "This painful time will pass."

"But no one will believe me, mom" I whined like a tired child. "I can't think of anything worse, than telling all the people I love that religion is just a scam."

"And yet, now that I've realized this, how can I not speak of it? How can intelligent people today, believe in human sacrifice or ever condone such a thing?"

"Don't be afraid, my darling, people will see this is very good news!" my mother gently assured, then disappeared into the ether.

Later, I tried to lift my spirits, hoping my illness would end, but the pain persisted relentlessly. I started to weep instead.

My mother returned the next morning and sat on the edge of my bed.

"Good morning," she cheerily greeted me, then she leaned closer in. "You need to write your book."

"Geez..." I whined, then wondered, "Is everyone in on this?"

So I remained in bed for a while, wondering what I might write. It needed to serve as a catalyst for independent thought, so by the end, the reader could truly hear their own unique voice.

* * *

That evening I bundled up to go for a walk before dusk, taking a snow covered path through the woods, along the edge of the lake.

As the moon rose up in the sky, I paused in admiration as it gently swooped down and silently walked beside me.

Spirit Moon was wearing the same little dress she wore in the summertime.

"Aren't you cold?" I asked.

"Not at all," she replied.

"Why not?" I responded to this.

"It isn't real," she wistfully said. "The cold is just an earthly illusion. In truth, it's perfect outside!"

* * *

Several weeks later, my abdominal pain continued to burn with striking intensity. It was amplified by the residual fear I held on a cellular level.

My kids were gone, my money was gone and my future felt like a mess. Despite the very best medical treatment, along with my clarity, it was hard to see past the pain.

But my Higher Self knew Spirit Moon was right, the physical world is illusion. In fact, it's comprised of 'Light' and the composition of all existence is cut from the same cloth.

Did you know, the average human body consists of seven octillion atoms giving off photons of light that our brains perceive as solid matter via the physical eye? But the existence of these charged particles as a material thing is just a collection of scientific probabilities.

Due to electromagnetic repulsion, every atom in existence is primarily empty space. So in many ways, the physical world is comprised of matter not unlike the twinkling stars in the heavens scattered throughout the void of space.

* * *

Everyday, I worked on clearing the hellfire in my first chakra. Some days felt better, some days felt worse and others were sheer misery. In fact, my condition brought to mind the cycle of human suffering.

That night, I quietly thought of the chief and what he would do in my place.

"Rise above it," I heard his encouraging words as my body's vibration increased. Soon I tingled all over and the pain had disappeared. The frequency shift was such a relief that I slept like a baby that night.

But the following morning, my doubts kicked in and the pain returned as before, so I emailed Marina for help.

Marina tuned in remotely and saw there were so many collective beliefs pouring into me that a "fiery transformational energy" was required to neutralize them.

"What you're experiencing is all about moving into a quiet, deep sense of peace," she explained. "And your Walk-In is having a facet change; an androgynous facet is coming in to create abundance for you."

"This will suppress your natural drive to have a mate right now, so you can fully focus on the divine task at hand. It will make romantic relationships elective for you instead, until you get to a place where you can have a magnificent one."

"Male and female paradigms will come to an end in the world, by bringing humanity's whole sense of self back into balance again with the reinstatement of the 'Divine Feminine' and 'Divine Masculine' energies within every human on Earth, fully merged into One."

I felt an enormous shift take place as the energies flooded my form, which awoke an acute awareness that many facets of myself had been dormant for thousands of years.

And with this, my power and sense of self no longer came from my mind, but from a limitless strength of the heart that replenished from within.

And so, I learned to be patient.

I learned to relinquish control.

I learned to trust the process.

I learned to trust myself.

I learned to trust my own unique vision of how my life would go.

And I learned to allow my creations to 'be'… knowing they would play out on their own.

Finally, I was at peace.

I would savor my life in this realm.

* * *

The next day, I stood in a vision on beautiful Sanibel. This was my sacred place on Earth. This was where I felt most connected to my Higher Self.

At least a dozen of my guides (frequencies of my unique consciousness) stood resolutely before me. They appeared to come from all over the world and some were other-dimensional.

My 'Healing Master' (a prevalent part of my divine consciousness) stepped forward from the group.

"You are here to liberate others from victimization on Earth," he explained. "You will help humanity reinstate their higher consciousness."

"That is your purpose now and your steps will be as follows; write your books and follow your guidance, you will be given signs."

I liked the simplicity of their plan, until it fully sank in.

"Wait. Did you say books?" I questioned. "I thought, I just had to write one?"

"It's your job to let go and completely believe," he said, ignoring my panic. "Have faith and remain steadfast within. Fully trust in your purpose. Your message will surely be well received and you will at last be heard."

Then he paused for a moment and looked deeply into my eyes.

"This is not elective," he said. "This is your destiny."

And with this, a Holy Bible appeared in his powerful hands.

"This is our gift to you," he said rather mysteriously, "and it will be your gift to the world," as he placed it in my heart.

"Now your only block to fulfilling your optimal destiny is your brain's need to be involved," he explained.

Instinctively, I folded my hands and placed them in front of my heart, then bowed toward this projection of my infinite consciousness as he placed his hands upon my head and neutralized my brain of any debris not aligned with my optimal destiny.

With all societal programming released from my energy grid, I saw my iridescent countenance as it truly is; infinite multidimensional presence made manifest here by Light.

"Now you have no physical programming blocking your clarity," he assured.

"You must have faith," added the voice of my own divine essence within.

"You must believe," I heard many guides coaching me as well.

As the book glowed deep within my heart as a gift from eternity, I knew this sacred narrative would become my destiny.

Later, I tried to understand what they had meant by this, so I found the well-worn bible my mother had left to me.

I began flipping through it, almost excitedly, looking for heavenly wisdom and the divine message therein.

But instead, I was shocked by the violence and suffering I found.

"Something's wrong," I thought as I continued to read. "I've only known God as forgiving and comprised of nothing but love."

"Yet everyone lives in extreme poverty as slaves, servants and soldiers, except for the merchants, rulers and priests."

"And the narrative barely acknowledges the existence of women at all."

"Perhaps, if I dig deeper, maybe I'll find some love or goodness buried within the text."

But the bible needed a karmic clearing, just like everyone else. Its energies were completely bogged down with violence, corruption and complete disregard for existence.

Was it really an ancient course that instills a state of fear?

Was it simply a tool to normalize greed and violence?

And is it meant to perpetuate the painful human condition?

Did you know, the bible has been rewritten more times than there are words written in it? Scholars will tell you this.

For example, between 1611 to 1769 it is estimated that church leaders, priests and scribes made over 24,000 changes to the Oxford edition alone to maintain their control over societies as the world evolved.

An example of an altered verse is John 14:6, which reads today, "I am the way and the truth and the life. No one comes to the Father, except through me."

Regarding this verse, the altered meaning suggests that worshipping Jesus Christ is the only way to heaven in the afterlife.

But via Simon's consciousness, I remembered, Jesus saying exactly the opposite.

Jesus originally said that "I am (being one's pure, divine self without any extra debris) is the way to the sacred truth (clarity) and the optimal life on Earth.

No one comes to a place in which they are truly self-actualized as their own inner authority (the father/mother-figure) except through the sacred 'me' - ie. by truly knowing themselves through their own divine consciousness.

Jesus was instructing us to grow up to be self-reliant as independent adults, so we're not dependent on others or duped by misinformation.

No first editions of the bible exist in the world today.

All original texts were destroyed by ancient authorities.

Did they destroy the originals to cover up the truth?

So I decided to read the book, from beginning to sacred end. And with this heartfelt intention, a heavenly process began as the words lit up on the pages that held the original truth.

The light-filled verses were mostly different from those written on the page and my heart swelled as the sacred truth revealed itself to me.

And I knew, I was seeing the remnants of what we had known as Essenes, if only intuitively.

Sacred truth is timeless and transcends all history.

So I recorded the luminous version of what the scripture once said and disregarded the rest of it as predatory illusion.

When I got to the end of it, I looked down at my notes and knew I was left with the same divine message, Jesus once talked about, portraying a higher perspective and the infinite wisdom of Source.

"Now, that's a much better bible!" I happily thought to myself.

* * *

Later, I met a friend for a walk and told him about my project and the engaging process therein. I had so much going on in my head that I chattered far too long.

"There are many ancient truths buried beneath the bible's text," I began. "In Genesis 1:26, the creation story once said, "Let us create humanity in our image after our true likeness... and so they created humanity in their own image, in the image of the gods (plural/gender neutral), they created everyone."

"But in contrast to this, religion promotes the idea of one supreme god."

"Was this their primary platform for global subjugation?"

"Humans were meant to care for the planet and every creature upon it. Vegetation was meant to nourish all humans and all creatures alike. No killing for food was intended."

"Was killing for food and sacrifice, one of the ways religion normalized violence in the world?"

"And what about the commandment, 'Thou shalt not kill'?"

"Why would God kill his only son and break his own commandment?"

"And aren't we all the children of god, so how are we any different?"

"And what about all the people who worship Jesus Christ?"

"Doesn't the first commandment say, 'Thou shalt have no gods before me'?"

"There are many contradictions in christianity, so I'm rewriting a different bible aligned with divinity."

As I finished my long-winded chatter, my friend thoughtfully paused, then responded transparently.

"The bible without the bullshit? Even I'd read that!" he said.

And together, we laughed at the truth of his irreverent honesty.

Chapter Eight

The Witness

Coffee in hand, I sat on the porch surveying the new spring growth as a past life aspect of a young boy, intuitively, came into view. I had once been a scout for my tribe, exploring neighboring islands in search of banana trees.

One day, I came upon some men, who had recently landed nearby, who captured me, beat me unconscious and took me far away.

For the next ten years, I was brutally forced to do various deeds for them. I lived in shackles and slept on the ground. I was treated with no dignity.

Years later, I knew their cruelty was bound to never end, so I smothered my drunken captor one night with the pillow next to him. At a very great price, I set myself free, then lived in quiet solitude, sad for what I had done.

This past life aspect had come into view to help me continue to heal. The undeserved trauma of his sad life had left residual pain and fear in my energy field.

I looked at my past life aspect and into his sorrowful eyes. I told him, he was a good man and that I was deeply sorry for the cruel injustice he'd endured in his life. I assured him, he was completely forgiven for his painful exit to freedom and that he deserved to cross over to peace, just like everyone else.

"Forgiveness is inherent in this system," I explained to him. "We are here to learn about love and learn to forgive ourselves."

So he accepted my explanation and walked into the light. Then, turning toward his reincarnation (me in this present life), he nodded a gentle "thank you" as he faded into the light.

Then nine other past life aspects appeared in front of me.

"You've got to be kidding," I thought, then wondered, if this healing process would ever come to an end.

First, was a pioneer woman, who had a hard life. Next, was a boy, who died very young, then seven more past life aspects lined up in front of me.

I acknowledged and thanked each one of them as they turned to go into the light, where the energies of their lives on Earth were fully neutralized.

Moments later, they reappeared bearing gifts they'd created in life, such as energies of compassion, fortitude, steadfastness, freedom and faith. All of these gifts and so much more came back to me in the present as the depth and breadth of their infinite wisdom filled me with heavenly light.

Then as the portal faded away, another appeared in its place.

"Now you have cleared your core residue," the higher realms explained. "So you are ready to bring your most significant aspect to light."

"Long ago, humanity lived in harmony with the world.

Humans watched over the planet, they cared for everything. As the guardians of the physical realm, they honored all existence."

And on that day, I met myself as an ancient medicine woman.

She was poised in the wilderness, sweetly smiling at me. When I asked where she lived, she spread her arms widely.

"Nature is home to me," she smiled, gazing upon all creation.

Together, we walked to a clearing, where deer had once bedded down for the night. A fire was briskly burning and we sat in front of it.

"Are you alone?" I asked, and wondered, if this was my fate.

"Not at all," the woman smiled at me as many people of varying ages appeared from the forest around us. They only possessed concepts of love and joy in their consciousness. They were nestled in a lush and remote valley somewhere in the Andes.

"So what's your role as a medicine woman?" I asked with curiosity.

Dotingly, she took my hand and led me back into the forest.

We walked along streams and through sunny meadows gathering herbs, berries and more, these are the life-force energies that provide wellbeing for all.

"This is the natural medicine that heals all creatures on Earth," she explained. "For every illness and imbalance, nature provides a cure. This is the inherent balance within dichotomy."

"Nature gives the body, mind and spirit all we need to be healthy and whole by regaining our balance in any case of dis-ease."

"Why is your life the most significant one for me in the present?" I asked.

"I am you, my dear one," she said admiringly. "We are One and the same, you and I. In fact, your present day incarnation is the reincarnation of me."

"You have traversed the wilderness of physical presence on Earth until you gathered all you needed to fully heal yourself. Now, you are whole and in balance again as your true authentic self."

"In fact, you have gathered more than enough to help others heal as well. Soon, you will live as a medicine woman and facet of Mother Earth."

"You need to trust and believe in yourself. You are channeling powerful love. You must allow your authentic presence to enlighten your energy field. You inherently have the support you need for a truly wonderful life."

And as our energies merged into One, I received the gifts from another past life and was calmed by her powerful presence.

* * *

Focused on personal healing, I had been pain-free for weeks. But with Easter, the pain returned with a mighty ferocity as layers of cellular programming reared their fiery heads.

Despite deeply rooted christian beliefs, my perspective had finally changed. The idea of human sacrifice was now appalling to me. How could any person today believe in such a thing? And the idea that humans should suffer, unless they subscribed to religion, felt predatory to me.

But the force of collective beliefs was conflicting with my truth, so my brain and cellular programming clashed with my knowingness as my first chakra (regarding my survival on Earth) flared in great distress.

So I focused on clearing my psyche of subjugating beliefs, hoping this would help. While doing so, I could see the image of St. Peter's crucifixion as held by one-third of the world and recognized this as another fear tactic and predatory illusion.

While journaling in bed that night, I dropped my pen on the floor. As I reached down to retrieve it, my first chakra pain disappeared, giving momentary relief.

Later that night as my pain increased, I tried an experiment, and discovered that when I turned upside down, my pain would go away.

So over the side of my bed I would flop when the pain grew too severe in a posture of total submission, replicating collective illusions of upside-down crucifixion.

Not long after, the chief appeared.

"What are you doing?" he asked.

I didn't respond to him.

"You must have faith," he suggested.

"I do," I grumbled back.

"No, you don't," he called my obvious bluff as he awkwardly turned upside-down himself to mimic my silly pose.

"What do you want from me?" I complained.

"You need to have faith in your destiny and fully trust in yourself," he said. "You can't give into collective fear or predatory illusion."

And with his reminder I realized, I needed to be strong, so I pulled myself upright on the bed with revitalized conviction.

* * *

At this point in my evolution, I consistently saw my body as comprised of sparkles of light; electromagnetic frequencies in evolving configurations.

Yet, as I looked at myself that day, I could see a contrast to this; the dark energies of collective programming were streaming into me and flooding my first chakra in an effort to be healed.

So I determined to free myself from being victimized. But as much as I tried to neutralize this, I couldn't keep up with the weighty energies streaming into me and greatly increasing my pain.

Despite this daunting dynamic, I sat up straighter yet.

"I'm not afraid of my path anymore and I won't be compromised," I announced. "I know, I am fully supported and I'm not giving up this time."

* * *

I awoke to the realization, I had fully assimilated the consciousness of Simon Peter on Earth. And I felt committed to bringing sacred truth back into the world, that we are all, without exception, divine presence while here.

In fact, we are nature itself.

We are the gods made manifest.

We are the image of Source.

We live our optimal lives in the present, while living from the heart.

I was also understanding more about Constantine's ancient scam, which has served as a popular prototype for subsequent predators.

Governments, corporations and other profiteers, similarly, plant fear in the masses with illusions of suffering, then promise them some relief in exchange for their personal freedom and wealth.

Are most institutions around the world just platforms for greed and corruption?

* * *

As time went on, I became less afraid of my own sense of sacredness. In turn, I became comfortable with speaking my own unique truth. I released all notions of suffering as inherent in our condition and committed to 'being' instead.

But right on cue the next morning, the lower realms called my bluff as my pain returned with a powerful and vengeful intensity. The following day was worse.

By early afternoon, I called on the chief for advice.

"Am I doing something wrong?" I asked my ethereal friend.

"Not at all," the chief replied.

"Then why do I continue to suffer?" I asked in a frustrated whine.

"You're clearing the way for others," he said. "It's part of the process, my dear one. In order to clear victimization from the human grid, cellular programming needs to be neutralized in the human form."

"You are the witness by which these vibrations are finally shifting on Earth. You are clearing your old beliefs and burning them out of your earthly form as an example for others."

"Okay," I said, rather tentatively. "As long as it makes it easier for others to do the same."

"It will," he confirmed.

Jesus was a prototype of 'that which we truly are.' He was without karmic buildup, weighing his psyche down. He exemplified pure human presence and clarity while on Earth.

* * *

I was focused on letting go of the grief that came with the loss of my mom. Gently, I let go of the pain from mistakes my mother had made, and as this layer of grief was released, I remembered my own mistakes as visions arose of many times, when I wasn't a perfect mom.

Tears welled as I thought of my failures regarding my precious children.

And from the ether around me, my children came into view, then lovingly draped themselves over me like a blanket of neutral compassion. Their sweet forgiveness encouraged me, at last, to forgive myself.

I silently wept as my past regrets released from deep within me.

As I lay down to sleep that night, I wondered, if I had more to release.

"Yes," I heard as a vision appeared of Jesus' crucifixion.

"What about Jesus not dying?" I asked.

"Let go of your fear regarding this knowledge," the higher realms advised.

"But I'm worried, I'll lose all the people I love," I confided in them.

"You need to give them more credit than that," they said regarding my fear. "Your message will surely be well received. It is very good news!"

* * *

A week later, I saw Marina.

As she tuned into my energy field, I could see the images too. I marveled at the realities, we can see intuitively, and how they manifest into form as the physical world.

Marina smiled at my thoughts as she scanned my energy field.

The primary sabotage, causing my pain, appeared as a wicked curse. It was rooted in my first chakra. It looked like a little black box filled with creepy, dark secrets securely locked within it.

It regarded my life as Simon and came from the Roman church.

"Does everyone have little black boxes of sabotage buried within?" I asked.

"Everyone has deep stuff to clear in order to bring in the new," she replied. "But you have extra to clear, because of the role you agreed to play in this present life."

Gradually, with our focused intention, the little black box was neutralized in my energetic form. Marina asked if there's anything else, I was ready to clear.

"No," we heard confirmation from the ether surrounding us.

But something didn't feel quite right, so I asked again.

"Is there anything I am ready to clear that's beyond this universe?

"Yes," came the affirmative answer, surprising both of us.

So we continued to clear my expanding energy field as other dimensions came into view in my ever-evolving awareness.

Then, we focused on healing my 'Self' that exists beyond this realm as more darkness continued releasing from my energy field.

"Is there anything left to clear beyond our ability to ask?" I wondered next.

"Yes," came the answer that made us laugh as we shook our weary heads, so we prayed for divine intervention.

The higher realms came in to clear all they could that day.

As they did, a tall, dark, hooded presence arose from my first chakra. This symbolized the veiled source of suffering on the physical plane and the source that perpetuates victimization in human consciousness that keeps humanity vulnerable to predatory illusion by holding human awareness captive at a very low vibration.

These other-dimensional energies were once harnessed by Constantine. They controlled the masses with the fear of pain by threatening their survival. And they remain the veiled energies commonly used today.

Quickly, my guides and higher support encapsulated the thing and whisked it off to a 'signature place' (a veiled, duplicate decoy with the same energetic signature that tricks the negative energy into thinking that it wasn't removed), where it couldn't do anymore harm.

"No wonder I haven't been able to get a date in so long," I joked.

"Seriously though, no wonder you've been in so much pain," Marina grimaced and laughed. "That was really creepy!"

The planet is purging the past, we have held onto for thousands of years. This is our reawakening; 'being' fully in the present, where reality truly exists.

We must let go of karmic buildup and foreign energies, so we can purge our subconscious mind of pain, fear, guilt, regret and human suffering.

We must fully 'be' in the present to live our optimal lives.

* * *

A week later, my pain had spiked rather dramatically, so I met with Marina one more time to clear it away for good.

After hours of searching, I turned upside-down for a while to relieve the pain. And from this posture, we realized, the source of my pain appeared to be coming from under the Vatican.

We were shown, the ancient necropolis where St. Peter's tomb still stands, isn't a tomb at all, but an altar corded to darkness from which the world's victimization began.

"It couldn't possibly be his tomb," I reacted to this. "Simon was never in Rome, it's all a bunch of nonsense."

We asked to completely disconnect me from the counterfeit tomb, then neutralized its off-planet source and completely shut it down.

As the altar was de-energized, Simon appeared next to me.

"I had nothing to do with this," he said emphatically.

"I know, I remember now," I replied.

"I just want it clear for the record," he said.

"What about the negative entities under the Vatican?" I asked. "They've victimized one-third of the world under the guise of religion."

"Now that their system is neutralized, they can't do any more harm and their purpose no longer exists, so they'll have to get better day jobs," Marina good-humoredly said.

"The planet will start a massive shift now that their system is gone and the church will go back to portraying Jesus as he really was, a prophet and gifted healer, who brought truth and light to the world. Soon, he will be remembered as the same divine essence inherent in all creation on Earth."

"We've all been duped by Constantine, but this should be the end," Marina confirmed.

"So what do I do now?" I thought.

"Move forward and follow the signs," Simon said. "Live your life as you truly are and embody the 'New Earth' energies streaming into the world, now that this system of victimization is finally at an end."

That sounded perfect to me.

"Wow, this is a very big day," I turned to Marina and said.

"Yes, it is," Marina replied. "And it looks like you have finally come through 'your dark decade' of the soul!"

We both laughed at this.

Simon stepped in a bit closer, clearer than ever before, as I noticed with great surprise that he was a version of me.

"These lower vibrations no longer exist energetically," he explained. "But we need to clear the residue from collective mind and bring back the many parts of ourselves they have stolen over time. Then we can fill our energy fields with our own divine essence again."

So we called in the collective souls, who would start the transformation by reclaiming the shattered pieces of their infinite consciousness.

And because I had served as a witness by which these systems would come to an end, we restructured my energy grid and released final residue.

Then Simon said, it was time for him to merge with me for good. And as he did, I re-membered another part of 'All That I Am' (Unified Consciousness).

His peaceful and powerful essence felt luminous to me.

"Simon has merged with your energy field to give you the faith and courage you had when you were him," Marina explained. "These energies will support your path in this present life."

And I realized, it's all about being authentic in every moment of life. It's about each of us simply being 'That Which We Truly Are.'

We evolve as needed, while living our lives in the physical realm. It's essential to love and forgive ourselves, so pain and fear are not retained on a cellular level. And when we live authentically, we create our very best lives.

I had completed my journey across the sacred bridge within. This is the journey of consciousness to complex, multidimensional presence and 'being human' again.

And the place in which I now live, known as 'The Sacred Heart' (a cosmic blackhole between everyone's 3rd and 4th chakras), is the portal through which we manifest our optimal presence on Earth.

* * *

Nicolaus Copernicus was a Renaissance-era mathematician, astronomer and catholic priest. In 1543, he published a groundbreaking heliocentric model of the universe that placed the sun, rather than the earth, at its center (despite the Greeks knowing this for thousands of years).

His radical findings debunked the geocentric model maintained by the church that the sun, moon, stars and planets all orbit around the earth.

In fact, his findings greatly challenged the infallibility of the church, which disempowered religious rule, and made belief in the church more elective and not a means of survival.

With the church's authority brought into question, countless doors and windows opened to a free-thinking world and this is how the modern scientific revolution began.

Over time, science displaced religion as western civilization's source of wisdom and truth.

But over the subsequent centuries, it would become glaringly clear that science is plagued with conjecture and self-serving agendas as well. Disappointingly, science has proven that it is not infallible either.

What other beliefs and societal programming keep us from knowing the truth?

* * *

Over the years, I continued to journal about many wonderful things. One morning, the Buddha appeared before me and looked deeply into my eyes.

"Namaste," we said as we placed our hands in reflective pose (palm to palm) and gently bowed our heads as our consciousness merged into One.

Then without warning, Siddhartha's presence gracefully merged with me. I was too stunned to react as I felt his energies fully aligning into 'that which I truly am.'

"I don't want to lose you again," I said in reaction to this.

"I am always with you, my friend," his voice now echoed gently within my infinite consciousness.

"But I want to be able to see you and I want to hold your hand," I reasoned like a child.

"My hand is now within your hand, where it will always be," Siddhartha comforted me.

And I knew, I would no longer see him as separate from myself, assured his loving and neutral presence would always remain with me.

When we allow neutrality to freely flow through ourselves, we are not the sum of the past.

Just as a small river can wash away the vast terrain, so can the flow of neutrality clear our subconscious debris, so we can be our optimal selves as awakened human beings.

* * *

As I tried to sleep that night, I wondered what would come next as Mother Earth appeared in the room and sat on the edge of my bed.

"Hi," I said to her beautiful image.

"Hi," she sweetly said back.

I wondered why she had appeared.

"Get up and write your book," she said.

"But it's the middle of the night," I tried to reason with her.

"Don't let minor inconveniences get in your way," she suggested.

* * *

I awoke the next morning and noticed something new - a divine, masculine presence was in my energy field.

As I adjusted to the change, I wondered why he was there.

Could this finally be 'the one' that I had been waiting for?

So I sat down in a quiet place, took a deep breath and turned within, then asked about this new man.

In a vision, we stood together, lovingly holding hands.

Later as he remained, I was puzzled about him again.

I assumed, I would see a past lifetime or something significant, but no other images came.

Chapter Nine

Shinkyo

As the weeks passed, the masculine presence steadfastly remained with me. He reminded me of Neo's vibe after breaking free from the matrix (the Wachowskis were way ahead of the curve when it comes to awakening).

Among the many dimensions in which we both seemed to be, a scene kept popping up that was rather surprising to me.

We stood together hugging and kissing with unabashed intimacy, while intermittently smiling and waving at my earthly presence.

We seemed to be excited to be seen by my present day self.

Again, I looked for a past life connection, but nothing was there at all. Yet the image remained with me, his presence unwavering, as he sent his support in a constant feed of empowerment to me.

And I knew he would continue to do this, until my personal power was equal to his own.

The following week, I met with my friends who had once been the Essenes. Together, we focused on clearing the matrices in collective mind that continue to smother the planet by neutralizing dichotomies, such as inequality.

When we finished the process, a Walk-In came in for me.

And with this, my previous Walk-In bowed with a sweet and gentle goodbye as a more advanced, ethereal presence joined me deep inside.

She appeared to be made of nothing but water - a facet of Mother Earth and 'nature intelligence' here.

Her gown looked like the ocean waves, her hair of flowing rivers and her energy field was a deep mountain lake with azure drops of rain.

Her elegant form was completely clear in a mix of turquoise and blue which made her completely invisible to the lower vibrations on Earth.

After several weeks of receiving his powerful frequency, I asked the masculine presence if there were any past lifetimes we'd shared.

He looked at me with a patient smile, then took me by the hand and led me to another dimension I wasn't aware of yet.

As we shifted into the 'Holy Dimension' where love is a sacred thing, our higher dimensional presence happily welcomed my earthly awareness.

They had been in this place together, since before the beginning of time as male/female counterparts on the ethereal plane.

And they smiled at me with knowingness of the beauty that is to come.

"So why is he staying with me, if we have no past lifetimes to clear?" I asked my higher awareness.

"To give you a pure and neutral connection through which you will channel true love," they replied.

"But I thought the higher realms don't really care about romance right now," I said, feeling rather indignant about how the Jake-thing turned out.

"Your contract is an exception to that as a part of awakening," they explained. "Your connection is higher dimensional and not from an earthly life. This is what you are witnessing in the higher realms; a unified and infinite love that exists beyond the physical world's programmed limitations."

"Once unified, you will help humanity rise above the paradigms that subjugate and objectify all creation in this realm. You will redefine love and beauty in a societal sense. This is the contract you have together, to exemplify sacred love."

I met Marina for lunch the next day.

"This might sound really weird," she said. "Did you know there's a higher vibrational entity in your energy field? He's super clear and perfectly centered in your sacred heart. In fact, he keeps projecting the image of 'Neo' from "The Matrix."

"He's been there, a while," I said with a laugh. "But I'm glad you're seeing him too. I was so surprised myself that I wondered, if he was real."

"Oh, he's definitely real," Marina said. "But it's important to remember that whatever we see intuitively is perceived through the unique filters in our energy fields. So although he looks like Neo, he's really the pure projection of your enlightened male counterpart as seen through your personal paradigm. He's the divine masculine presence inherent in your Walk-In."

"In the Holy Dimension, you've been one another's reflection long before time. You are becoming whole again, by merging your multidimensional consciousness into one unified soul, so you will no longer be limited by the fractured sense-of-self we experience in the physical realm at this time in the world."

"These higher dimensional counterparts are meant to work as a team. You'll be comprised of a water vibe (divine feminine presence) and you'll equally be of the air (divine masculine presence).

In fact, it looks like your Walk-In has already merged with you and now you're matching these frequencies, we attribute to Mother Earth.

And once your water and air elements fully assimilate, they will create the perfect storm to help humanity heal."

I noticed that my new Walk-In was not only a water vibe, but a blend of all of the lives I am living in other dimensions right now that give me the tools for my earthwork as they gently flow in and out of my presence just like the changing tide.

* * *

I finally felt at peace with the paradigm shifts I had made, regarding my life as Simon.

"It's nice to know that Jesus wasn't really tortured to death and that he died quite peacefully much later in his life," I said.

"I couldn't agree more," said Marina.

"You know what else?" I continued. "It's shocking, how I used to accept all the religious stuff I was taught. As a child, I was told we're all sinners and inherently flawed, innocently never questioning, if it was true or not."

"As a teen, I studied the catechism, so I could be confirmed and participate in the ritual of holy communion in church; symbolically drinking Christ's blood every month and eating a piece of his flesh."

"But isn't that cannibalism or something even worse? Seriously, when you think about it, how totally creepy is that?"

"And what's with the symbol of a cross being a positive thing?" I asked. "Crucifixion was used by governments to torture and terrorize humans, yet people hang them in their homes and wear them as jewelry?"

Then I paused for a moment and spoke in a mischievous tone.

"Maybe I should design a bracelet with torture devices as charms, like cute little crosses, guillotines, stockades, hangman's nooses... oh, and electric chairs!"

"Gross!" Marina said, laughing. "But you know, it's actually true that organized religion can twist our point of view."

"Take the sign of the cross, for example. Making the sign of a torture device across your energy field is really a type of encoding that blocks awareness of sacred truth and inherent connection with Source."

Marina made the sign of the cross with a line from her head to her heart (connecting the two energetically), then another line from shoulder to shoulder (severing that connection). And after her demonstration, she quickly shook it off.

"Wow, you're right!" I exclaimed as the encoding lit up in my face. "I never realized the sign of the cross blocks our heart connection."

"Before Constantine's time, a symmetrical cross was symbolic of love for all presence on Earth," Marina explained. "It's the Council of Nicaea that pulled it out of whack as a symbol of torture to intimidate everyone."

* * *

For more than a decade, my sacred place had been on Sanibel, but the next day during my meditation, a surprising shift occurred.

My Higher Self stood in the mountains just west of Los Angeles, gazing over the ocean along the Pacific West Coast.

I didn't welcome this change at all, so I tried to shift my sacred place back to Sanibel, but every time I bounced right back as if magnetically pulled.

In addition to this, I didn't look ethereal anymore, I just looked like my normal self (when viewed intuitively).

Was this the kind of sign that Simon had talked about?

Then I abruptly let go and gave in as I noticed the cool ocean breeze and loved the sensation of it.

"The winds of change are upon us," I thought.

"Oh, how I love the wind!"

* * *

One day, I asked, if someone like 'Neo' would be my partner in life.

"No," came the answer loud and clear, so I tried a different approach.

"Could someone with these energies appear when the time is right?"

"In a way," came the answer I'd hoped for, but then I instantly knew, the image of Neo symbolized the missing half of myself, and wasn't the representation of any one else in the world.

And with the assimilation of my divine counterparts (male and female in balance), I would be fully restored as unified presence on Earth.

And with the reinstatement of my unified consciousness, I would attract my optimal version of 'Neo' in this realm, as like attracts like and water finds it's own level.

Instantly, my monkey-mind chattered, questioning my self worth.

"Enough!" thundered the chief from afar. "We are all worthy of love."

* * *

As the months passed, my Higher Self remained on the west coast. There was no denying it, I was drawn to Los Angeles. So I packed my bags one day and said goodbye to my friends.

I traveled along the Canadian border and crossed the Rocky Mountains. From there, I drove down the famous and windy Pacific West Coast to see the great sequoias, I had learned about as a child.

'The Avenue of the Giants' was far better than I could have hoped. The ancient trees seemed to welcome me as I got out of my car.

Amidst these magnificent conifers, I was filled with wonder and awe, then unexpectedly, heard their voices audibly speaking to me.

"Dear One," they got my attention. "Run your own unique energies as tall as the sequoias and as expansively rooted. Be true to yourself in every regard. This will make you completely stand out as a giant among the masses, who are currently watered-down."

"Thank you," I said to the great ones, then fervently hugged those nearby.

And while standing among the great sequoias, a paradigm shift began.

Is all existence consciousness?

Is consciousness all that I am?

Does the consciousness of all existence create reality here?

'Consciousness' was the concept by which I now defined myself. Past life aspects (personalities), various facets of ourselves (multidimensional presence) and our Higher Selves (our unique, unified energy matrix) all move in and out of our presence as needed while on Earth.

But the energy of divine consciousness is 'That Which I Truly Am' in any place and time, and the consciousness of 'All' combined is the substance we know as Source.

Source is the energy we become as Unified Consciousness.

* * *

When I moved to Los Angeles, I was still in rough shape. I couldn't digest food very well, along with some other things.

During a walk on the beach one day, I thought of the $84 that remained in my bank account, after several months of job hunting, nothing had panned out.

"What's the point?" I asked with annoyance.

Had my move been a big mistake?

Then in a vision, I witnessed the story of Jesus walking on water, while Simon (afraid of the changing wind) was panicked and starting to sink.

"Seriously, you're throwing that in my face?" I challenged the heavens above as the story's lesson, "with faith, all things are possible," broke into my wavering mind.

Then as I looked out over the ocean, something came into view as I saw beyond the fear in my mind and into a possible future.

There upon the water stood my divine male consciousness, encouraging me to walk on the water, by rising above the fear in my head and expanding my perspective.

As I continued to watch the scene, the wind began to roar, as a facet of my present day self appeared on the water as well, nodding with affirmation that I was already there.

And the countless configurations of my infinite soul smiled throughout the ether.

With this vision of walking on water, I saw a future world in which love and honor are all that exist while living our lives on Earth.

And with this new experience, a change within me occurred.

As I walked home from the beach that day, 'my sacred place' was no longer the place where I stood in the physical realm, but instead, it arose from the depths of my soul as a portal of physical presence.

'I AM' my sacred place in the world and I am what makes it so.

* * *

Despite all of my realizations, I still wasn't sure about life, so I looked up to the heavens one day, and asked to know the 'Truth.'

"The image of God you hold in your mind does not exist," I heard. "It is an earthly illusion."

"What?" I thought. "That can't be true. I met God on the ethereal plane and he held me in his arms."

Then I remembered, how I had learned to imagine God as a child.

One night, when I was 4 years old and learning how to pray, I knelt beside my toddler bed and folded my little hands. But I didn't know how to envision the God, who would be hearing my prayer.

"I don't know what he looks like," I confessed to my doting mom.

"Pretend he's a heavenly king on a throne," my mother lovingly said.

Innocently, I embellished him with a fancy robe and a crown. And that was the image of God I had cherished over the subsequent years.

"Who was standing before me on the ethereal plane, when I 'knew' I was seeing God?" I challenged their blasphemy.

"The pure and perfect image of your 'Unified Sacred Self' that's comprised of all that exists," my guides explained to me.

"The image of God you witnessed was the presence of all life force energies channeled into 'One' as seen through your personal paradigm. But in contrast to this, Source is the unification of all that exists (without programming or debris)."

Not sure what to think, I searched the etymology of 'God' on my phone and was surprised to learn, the concept of 'God' is a relatively modern term.

It was coined in the Middle Ages by scribes translating the bible from German into English.

The earliest form of the German word 'gott' comes from the 6th century 'Codex Argenteus.'

It was never capitalized nor was it gender specific; it was a neutral term.

Earlier roots of the English word 'God' come from Old Saxon, Sanskrit and Proto-Indo-European languages.

It originally meant 'to invoke,' 'to call upon,' 'to unite' or 'to join.'

And I realized, the concept of 'God' as we think of it today, is very different from what it meant before Constantine's time.

In fact, the original concept meant 'to call upon a unified presence' just like collective mind.

Later, I called Marina, who confirmed this point of view.

She understood 'the collective' to be the presence of God in the world.

Then, I asked the chief what he thought.

"The Ancestors are not separate, they are One in the heavens," he said. "I am One and I am many. The Creator is here as each of us, while comprised of all that exists."

And with this, I felt more comfortable, but still wasn't sure what to think. I much preferred a 'Supreme Being' taking care of me.

So I asked for help in adjusting to what this was really about as a host of beautiful presence appeared to show their loving support.

"Who and or what is really God?" I asked the heavens that day as a plethora of sacred descriptors flooded my energy field.

"I am that I am," says the Hebrew Bible in Exodus 3:14.

"I will be what I will be" in Exodus 3:12.

"I will be" or "I shall be" is written in Genesis 26:3.

While the Latin tetragrammaton 'YHWH' (Yahweh) is 'God' in the Hebrew Bible, which simply means "to be," "to exist," "to cause to become" or "to come to pass" as the "breath of life" in the world.

"I am that I am" is the Hellenistic Greek translation of God, while "I am that which is" stands for God in the Greek Old Testament.

And according to Philo of Alexandria, a Jewish philosopher, Exodus 3:14 translates: "I am the being that, when they have learned the difference between 'being' and 'that-that-is-not,' they may know there is no name whatsoever that can be assigned to 'Me' to whom only belongs 'existence'."

Revelations 1:8 declares, "I am the Alpha and the Omega, the beginning and the end, the 'be' and the 'was' and the 'is to come'."

Finally, according to Advaita Vedanta, a South Indian philosophy, out of all the descriptions of 'God' in the world, the Biblical statement, 'I AM THAT I AM' is the most accurate as an esoteric abstraction that the human mind can grasp, aptly describing the 'stateless state' of the 'absolute' and 'supreme reality' defined as 'awareness without any thought, emotion, perception, association and/or memory.'

And I noticed that all these descriptions didn't mention a king on a throne, a father, a judge or a ruler of any kind at all.

Nor was God gender specific, but 'that which is invoked' and 'beyond describable.'

Furthermore, I now realized that the greatest sage of all, who said it better than all sacred texts, "May the force be with you" was Yoda.

And as I adjusted to all of this, I realized something more. 'The Sacred Word' is not a book nor any religious text, but a reference to 'intention put forth' as sacred in this realm.

With every thought, word and deed vibration flows into the world as a ripple of powerful frequencies creating reality here.

And collective intention put forth en masse transforms the state of the world.

So take care and know you create your life with every thought, feeling and word.

* * *

I awoke the next morning, feeling overwhelmed. A loop of old karmic baggage had released from my energy field.

It was almost too much to handle.

"Believing in karma and other illusions housed in the physical mind is distracting your attention," the chief said, raising his voice. "You have to stop wasting your time!"

"What?" I responded, blankly.

"Remember the black moon, my dear one," he said to his blossoming child.

"What?" I repeated, completely confused.

"You heard me," the chief encouraged.

Then I remembered the black moon from my aboriginal lives.

That night, I made my way home from the beach as the moon rose up in the sky and Spirit Moon came to visit me, one last time.

I hadn't seen her in over two years, since living up north with my dad and noticed, with great surprise, that she was no longer a child.

"How did you grow up so quickly?" I asked.

"I haven't changed at all," the knowing spirit replied. "You are the one who has changed, while I remain the same."

Then I remembered the black moon has no light of its own, it only reflects the sun.

"The black moon is the ethereal moon," Spirit Moon explained. "I reflect the light of Source, so my image is your ethereal form, when seen through intuitive eyes."

Now, I knew the beautiful presence walking next to me was really my own celestial image reflected to me as the moon. I was the one who'd self-actualized over the past two years as my journey to 'being human' again was fully realized.

Then we smiled at one another and gracefully merged into One as I continued to unify my awakening paradigm.

* * *

Over the months my vibration increased. I created a meaningful life, surrounded by wonderful friends. As I connected with various people, I easily recognized them as visions of previous cycles on Earth became apparent to me.

We haven't evolved energetically as science may suggest. We've 'devolved' as beings of consciousness by rooting ourselves in the physical mind and forgetting our sacredness.

We are all divine beings immersed in a human experience.

Marina called the following day as something quite striking lit up.

"You're in an ascension process," she said. "This is your final lifetime in the physical realm. You are becoming an 'Ascended Master' during your time on Earth."

"That's why this particular life has been so intense for you. You can return to this realm if you want, but you're finished with your own evolution, once this life is through."

"Cool, but weird," I responded as my monkey-mind kicked in.

"But I'll miss my kids," it chattered at me, not quite sure about this.

Then I saw my children and loved ones smiling and waving at me from many other dimensions, less arduous than Earth.

And I knew we are all the ancients of the physical realm, seeded by the Pleiades a very long time ago.

I was completing my fourth cycle here to evolve as collective mind and knew, I'd been returning to Earth for many millions of years.

* * *

A lot of human perception has been lost or gotten off track. For example, Constantine duped the masses for nearly 2,000 years.

And the physical mind has been programmed by various entities to perceive the world in a mixed up, muddled up, limited fashion, indeed.

As I wondered what other nonsense was floating around out there, the image of a dinosaur, intuitively, came into view and something about their history no longer rang true for me.

Dinosaurs were discovered in the mid-19th century by Sir Richard Owen of England. He coined the term 'dinosauria' in 1842 as the "distinct suborder of saurian reptiles" found all over the world.

But there's universal consensus among paleontologists today that birds are descended from dinosaurs, not reptilian babes.

There is also debate as to whether or not all dinosaurs were winged, though evidence of winged dinosaurs is surprisingly overwhelming.

Dinosaurs had complex systems of air sacs, similar to that of birds, that pumped air into vast hollow cavities and lots hollow bones, thereby making them very lightweight and well-suited to flying around.

They also had high metabolisms, creating exceptional heat, that vented through these avian systems, enabling them to give off exhaust at extremely high degrees.

Then I wondered, why these massive creatures weren't discovered in earlier times, while the fabled dragon was often portrayed in ancient legends and art.

Where were the earlier references about all the dinosaurs?

Could the science community have misled the entire world with another self-promoting theory, they've peddled to us as real?

For example, could the dinosaur fossils in all the museums today, really be the bones of the not-so-fabled dragon?

* * *

I awoke the next morning, thinking of Jesus again.

I thought about human history and how it can be altered as a story is passed around.

Then I began to wonder if 'Jesus' was really his name.

'Haeland' (meaning 'healer') was his Old English name. 'Iesous' was the Greek rendition and root of the English name 'Jesus' (coined in the 12th century) some of us use today.

But Jesus wasn't an Englishman nor was he ever Greek.

In fact, in his native Hebrew, his name was something like 'Yeshua' which translates into 'Josh.'

So I sat down in a quiet place, took a deep breath and turned within.

"What was Jesus' real name?" I asked as his image appeared.

"Yehoshua ben Yosef," I remembered his true name.

"Yehoshua," I repeated, just to hear it again.

We had called him by his formal name, he was 'Joshua' in English.

And as we smiled at one another, I looked into his eyes and knew the image before me was the best friend I'd ever had.

Then his image began to shift and rose up as ethereal light. I remained completely transfixed as his energies merged with my own. I would no longer look upon him. We were now as One.

Again, I thought of the telephone game, I used to play as a child. Even his name had been altered as the stories were passed around. No wonder, the truth about his life had gotten so twisted around.

* * *

Over time with various revelations, my confidence slowly grew, until I summoned the courage to finally write a book.

But with my clear intention, my monkey-mind chattered at me.

"They're going to think, I'm crazy," it screeched. "And it's going to be all your fault. You're going to lose the people you love and you're going to piss everyone off!"

So I calmed my monkey-mind with the reassuring words, I once heard from the sequoias.

"Run your own unique energies as tall as the sequoia and as expansively rooted," I reminded my busy brain, then saw myself as a giant now too, as 'That Which I Truly Am.'

"It's going to be okay," I said to my noisy mind. "You know what we've seen, where we've come from and who we really are. The truth of what awakening brings, isn't that big of a deal. It's just about being true to yourself and that which you've been all along."

"Okay. Here goes!" I thought to myself as my mind began to cringe.

So I sat down in a quiet place, took a deep breath and turned within as I opened my laptop to write…

There's a sacred bridge called Shinkyo, leading from the city of Nikko to Futarasan Shrine, a Shinto Temple founded in 8th Century Japan.

There you will find an ancient relic, known as a Shinkyo too, a sacred mirror symbolizing Honesty, Wisdom and Truth.

As the legend goes, hermit-priest Shodo Shonin was on a pilgrimage to climb Mt. Nantai, when he came upon the torrential Dayo River.

Unable to go any farther, he lit a fire and asked the gods to assist him with his crossing.

Out of the heavens descended two beams of golden light over which he traversed the uncrossable torrent to establish the sacred place there.

Since the moment I first crossed Shinkyo as a teacher in my youth, I've had a deep affinity for this elegant little bridge, along with the double metaphor of the sacred mirror within.

And perhaps the journey of Shodo Shonin is not unlike my own, from the physical mind to the sacred heart, where I see my unique reflection as 'That Which I Truly Am.'

Across this sacred bridge, I have traveled to the portal of light within, where there is no veil between Heaven and Earth, where all existence is One.

And this is where I now reside with the living spirits on Earth. They are you, they are me, they're complex, multidimensional beings, perfect in every way, comprised of infinite consciousness, they are shaping reality.

We can all make this sacred journey. We are equally divine. Just follow your own inner voice, it's the voice of the gods resonating within. It will guide you to your own unique truth and to being human again.

May the Source be within you…

…as it has always been!

The graphic above is the 26th character 'ghan' in the Georgian alphabet. It was the symbol of love and the heart, before Constantine's time. It shows the heart as open, while living our lives on Earth, unlike the symbol today. May it trigger your own unique journey to being human again.

www.ingramcontent.com/pod-product-compliance
Lightning Source LLC
LaVergne TN
LVHW051728080426
835511LV00018B/2948